Frugal Yachting

Frugal Yachting

Family Adventuring in Small Sailboats

Larry Brown

International Marine
Camden, Maine

Published by International Marine®
10 9 8 7 6 5 4 3 2 1

*Library of Congress Cataloging-in-
Publication Data*
Brown, Larry, 1946-
    Frugal yachting : family adventuring in small
sailboats / Larry Brown
        p.   cm.
    Includes bibliographical reference and index.
    ISBN 0-07-008247-2
    1. Sailing.   2. Family recreation.   I. Title.
    GV811.B714   1994
    797.1'24—dc20   93-40391
                                              CIP

Questions regarding the content of this book
should be addressed to:
    International Marine
    P.O. Box 220
    Camden, ME 04843

Questions regarding the ordering of this book
should be addressed to:
    TAB Books
    A Division of McGraw-Hill, Inc.
    Blue Ridge Summit, PA 17294
    1-800-233-1128

Printed by Arcata Graphics, Fairfield, PA
Design by Faith Hague
Production and page layout by Janet Robbins
Edited by Jonathan Eaton, Kathy Newman, and
Pamela Benner

To my parents, from whom I learned the love of sailing. . . to my children Julie and Amber. . . and to Bettina for being the fellow voyager I had always dreamed of.

Contents

Part V   The Boats   92

Preface

It seems like so long ago. I had gone driving on a bitter November afternoon when my path took me by a boat shop. Sitting on the lawn was a Com-Pac 16—what was then a brand-new product. I'd always had what seemed to me the romantic idea of a little ship that was tiny, yet complete, and there it was parked by the side of the road. The shop was open and soon I was in the cabin, snuggling into one of the bunks, imagining where everything would go. Alas, the boat was new and I couldn't afford it. (Shortage of funds was the other main theme of my entry into boating.) I returned home with a brochure, which I have kept all these years. I had the ache and would have to figure out what to do about it. Now I can tell you, dear reader, that the ache is not terminal—but it is chronic.

I began to collect information on small boats from around the country, using *SAIL* magazine's annual directory as a springboard.

Soon I had a lot of information and was beginning to draw my own conclusions. I wished someone else had done this earlier and written a book for people looking to buy their first boat. Since there was no such book, I wrote my own: *Sailing on a Micro-Budget*. Over the years, boat companies have come and gone; the market and its products have evolved; and my family and I have traveled widely—and learned a lot. It seemed time to go over the book and see what was still true and what needed to be added or changed. *Frugal Yachting* is a longer book—a better book than I could have written in the late 70s when I had just started my project.

Some things haven't changed: We still have to make every penny count; we still prefer small boats. Since there is a certain risk attached to lusting after material objects—even boats—we are better off keeping our designs modest. We barely fit into our boats, but our boats fit neatly into our larger concerns: our marriages, our plans for the family, our time, our budgets, our desire to experience nature while leaving her undisturbed. In the end, the mission of this updated and expanded volume is still the same: to share with you what I've learned, to talk to you in print as comfortably as if you were sitting in the cockpit with me . . . and to reflect with you occasionally about what this passion for the water means.

Frugal Yachting

Part I

The
Invitation

The Possibilities

The last time we sailed into the harbor at West Falmouth, Massachusetts, our camera was on the fritz and so we missed taking an odd and informative picture. Let me paint it for you.

In the center of the frame, you see our little sailboat, *Fearless*, floating in a sea of crystal blue. In the background, slightly out of focus, is the stone breakwater that shelters West Falmouth from Buzzards Bay. Two children appear to be walking across the surface of the water toward the boat, one carrying a horseshoe crab the size of a dinner plate, the other gesticulating wildly with her arms. Those are our daughters, Julie and Amber.

"How have we trained our children to walk on water?" you ask. We haven't. They're standing on the bottom. That sailboat, our floating home for the weekend, draws only 7 inches! You'll notice ours is the only boat in the picture. That's because there isn't another cruising boat in West Falmouth that would dare come in here—or that wouldn't run aground long before it got here. It's a delightful spot and we have it all to ourselves.

Now let me turn my back on my family and on our little sailboat and take another picture, this one of West Falmouth Harbor. I'll need a telephoto lens because we are, as I've explained, rather far from it. West Falmouth, with some fine old homes ranging along the shoreline, is a lovely corner of Buzzards Bay. In its sheltered harbor you'll see, from our vantage point, a small forest of masts. These masts are connected to a small fleet of some beautiful and expensive cruising boats that rest peacefully at their moorings. You'd think that these boats would be a hub-

bub of joyful activity: kids swimming and splashing and sails rattling up the masts . . . but no. There isn't a soul around. All is strangely tranquil. From time to time you'll see some kids slide a Beetle Cat off the sand and go sailing. Still, it's odd that there's so much here and so little going on. What's even stranger is that, at this moment, similar fleets lie idle across the bay in Marion, in Mattapoisett, at Onset—millions of dollars worth of yachts just sitting at their moorings. Don't be alarmed. Nothing's wrong; nothing has happened. This is normal. Most of these boats are rarely used. Surely they're enjoyed when they *are* used. But the rest of the time they are simply floating symbols—distant Tarzan yells—announcing the financial potency of their owners.

Well, I'll make a confession. I don't have any financial potency. I'm a teacher and my income is modest to an embarrassing extreme. If you can afford to buy this book, you probably make more money than I do. But I've got a boat. We make voyages. We're out sailing and the millionaires are not. What's our secret? I'll tell you. The answer is the subject of this book. Basically it's this: We're out here sailing and swimming because we didn't spend a lot of money on our boat. We couldn't afford to buy a yacht, so we didn't. We have a little 15-foot boat with a cabin and a boom tent over the cockpit and we make do. And we have fun.

Let me share with you a fairly well-kept secret. It's so often true we could almost call it a law: The use a boat gets is in inverse proportion to its size and cost.

If you're not wealthy and you want to go sailing and cruising, you can. My boat cost a little less than four thousand dollars, trailer and everything, brand new. Used boats cost less. Don't assume that the family with the $40,000 yacht is going to have 10 times the fun you will. They won't. You may actually do more sailing, and have more fun, than they—with far fewer worries. Real "riches" are measured not in what you own, but in what you can do.

What *can* you do with a small sailboat? If hardship, discomfort, and solitude turn you on, you can cross an ocean in a small boat. It's been done dozens of times now. If you don't mind roughing it a bit you can cruise along thousands of miles of coastlines, exploring hidden waterways out of the reach of larger craft.

With thorough and realistic planning, you can bring your family. Here's a chance for real adventure without the solitude. You can easily haul your lightweight boat overland and put it where you actually want to be, leaving the extended (and often tiresome) passagemaking for boats too heavy to follow suit. Whereas the deeper and heavier yacht has to lie offshore, you can sail right up to a beach and go exploring. Often you can set up tents and camp ashore overnight, adding a whole new dimension to your cruising.

If you're a cruising couple, you can enjoy a degree of privacy unavailable to large coastal cruising yachts. You can sneak into tiny coves and inlets too shallow for deeper boats and have them all to yourselves. Here's your chance for a naked moonlight plunge without entertaining a whole fleet of nosy neighbors. You can trailer your boat to places off the beaten path and away from the crowds, find an unoccupied island and play Adam and Eve for an afternoon—or a weekend. If you're young and money comes hard, you're in luck. You won't need too much and you can do it now while you have energy and freedom of movement to take

best advantage of what small-boat cruising has to offer.

Here are some sample cruising plans you could do, depending on where you live:

- You're a family of four living in Albany, New York. In the spring, you trailer your used 22-foot family weekender to a marina on beautiful Lake Champlain. You bought the boat in 1989 for $7,000. Off and on during the summer you drive up to your boat, safely stored ashore at a marina, launch it at the marina's ramp, and go sailing. After your weekend cruise is finished, you haul the boat out again, park it ashore, and drive back to Albany. You aren't hauling it around all the time; Lake Champlain is easily big enough to keep you interested all summer, and you've saved the cost of a slip or a mooring by launching the boat only when you need it. In the fall, you haul the boat back home and store it for free in your backyard. Next year maybe you'll do the same thing on Lake George, or on Lake Ontario, or on the Hudson.
- You're a doctor, living on Long Island. Each year, your family enjoys swimming at your family cottage on the sound. You've purchased a 16-foot sloop, new for $6,500, and moored it a few dozen yards offshore. The boat has a small cabin with two bunks and a portable toilet. Most of the time you daysail the boat and use the cabin for changing in and out of bathing suits, going to the bathroom, and as a safe playpen for visiting friends with small children. You and your wife have snuck out overnight a few times. Once, even though it was cramped in the cabin, you made love in there and then went for a midnight swim. You felt like kids again. Speaking of kids, your two boys

have been campaigning to get your consent. . . . They want to go on a week's cruise to Mystic, Connecticut, and back. They are 16 and 13 and they're good sailors. The little boat seems safe enough and they really want to do it. You think maybe the next time they ask, you'll say yes.

• You're a young couple in Phoenix, Arizona. You've only been married a year and, though you're both working, money is scarce. You've found a used cabin sloop only 14 feet long for $3,200. It has a reputation for making voyages of impressive distances and the two of you are intrigued. Your wife used to go canoeing and both of you are experienced backpackers.

After a season of happy sailing on some of the nearby desert lakes, you're planning trips to the Sea of Cortez. If that goes well, you might even take a year off work and sail the Gulf of Mexico from Mexico to Florida, exploring and occasionally working odd jobs along the way. Your parents think you're both nuts, but you know you're not.

• You're retired and living with your husband in Florida. You've always loved sailing and have owned several boats over the years from 27 to 41 feet. Now you want something very light and simple. Several companies not far from you manufacture boats about 17 feet long with comfortable berths and room for a modest galley that cost between $7,000 and $9,000.

Your kids, remembering the luxury of your earlier boats, can't picture you in something so compact. They think you're crazy, but you know you're not.

• You're a student at the University of Oregon. You and two of your fraternity brothers have fixed up an old fishing dory and you're planning to spend the summer sailing and camping around Vancouver Island. You each have solo tents and backpacks. You figure the trip will cost $300 apiece—maximum. The boat cost you $100.

• At a boat show last winter, you fell in love with a 16-foot sailboat and surprised your family by driving home with it. Your wife is unmoved by your excuse that it was a steal at the boat-show price. Now you're sitting with everybody at the dining room table with a road atlas spread out. With a magic marker you're circling all the places you can go cruising. You were beginning to agree with your wife that you had made a very costly mistake, but no longer. There are bunches of places to go sailing within driving distance of your house. Your kids are excited; your wife is slowly coming around, too. This is going to be even more fun than you thought.

A working family, a professional man, two newlyweds, a retired couple, three college students. . . all of them can enjoy most of the same pleasures as an affluent yachtsman:

Freedom: An escape from the ordinary world, the opportunity to follow the wind and leave your wristwatch at home.

Adventure: The thrill of exploring new places, experiencing the unexpected and taking as many personal risks as you are willing to take.

Romance: The visceral joy of a tanned body, warm water, sunsets, waves lapping against the hull. . . .

Luxury: Here you and the yachtsman part company. For him, boating means pressurized water, electric lights—maybe even a shower on board—and a mortgage as hefty as the one on your home. For you, it means a warm place to lie down, a camp stove, a bath in the water you sail in, new cruising waters every time if you want, minimum financial investment, little risk, and no worry.

Freedom, adventure, romance. These can all be yours if you can do without the luxury, once you stop thinking of your boat as a status symbol and start thinking of it instead as a ticket to freedom.

Who Owns What?

In a meadow in Fairhaven, Massachusetts, lies the hull of a 27-foot sailboat. It's one of those kit jobs you can buy with the fiberglass hull already completed. All its owner had to do was build the plywood interior, rig mast, and sails and go. It's half-finished and the man is exhausted, sick of it. He's put much more time and money into the job than he expected and he can't go on. He also can't get out. If he sells the boat as is, he'll lose his shirt. If he hires someone else to finish it, he'll have to ask more than it'll be worth. He doesn't have the boat, the boat has him.

A boyhood chum of mine and his wife went sailing on my 14-foot West Wight Potter. They loved it. A year later I had moved up to a 22-footer, and after a weekend aboard that boat they were hooked. They bought a 33-foot Hunter, convinced they could defray the boat's expenses by chartering it. My friend is an astute businessman and so he's off to a good start.

We went sailing the first summer on their new acquisition. The big boat absorbed five adults and a child with ease. Here was a boat you could really live on! But the previous charter customer had left the pressure on in the alcohol stove and, when my friend leaned against it, it swung on its gimbals and dumped an astonishing quantity of explosive fuel onto the cabin sole. Then the first mate forgot to turn the pressure off on the head and soon water was flooding the toilet compartment. Finally we got underway and, with our enormous draft, had to motor up the channel for the best part of an hour while all around us smaller sailboats zoomed around wherever they liked.

This year my friend is tired. His wife is getting sick of hearing about boats and he's sick of not being able to sail. Suddenly his pride and joy has become a trap. If he lowered his boat into one of the local Pennsylvania lakes, the water level would probably rise 3 inches. If he just sailed the boat and forgot the charter business, he'd go broke. If he chartered it all season long, he'd turn a small profit and he'd also go nuts. He doesn't have the boat any more, it has him.

What's going on here? My friend himself summed it up: "I forgot what it was I really wanted. I really wanted to go sailing, to be on the water, to go to sleep hearing the waves lap against the hull. But I got distracted. I started comparing boats and got involved in all the features these boats had. I started falling in love with boats instead of with sailing."

There's a funny paradox here. Certainly you can't go sailing without a boat, yet if you start thinking more about the *object* than you do about the *activity,* something starts to go wrong. You become a materialist.

Your spouse, with an unerring nose for

trouble, begins to hate the boat and its intrusion into your heart.

"How can anyone be jealous of a thing?" you ask. "Easily," I reply, as one who knows. We fall very easily into love with things. It's not good for us.

Here's my advice; it's the underlying premise of this book: Think minimum. Buy something that costs less than you can afford. Accept the challenge. Find ways to make do. Don't borrow money for it. Don't get anxious about it. Keep it fun. J. P. Morgan was correct when he said, "If you have to ask how much it is, you can't afford it." Arrogant, but right. By all means go sailing. Escape to the thousands of rivers and lakes and bays and estuaries and ocean beaches this country and its neighbors have to offer. Swim, sail, let your boat drift, and feel the sun on your body; camp aboard or ashore and sleep under the stars. Explore a different waterway every time you go out. But keep it simple. Don't overinvest. Mountain climbers carry all their needs on their backs. Why should you need more? Go sailing. Then, when you return, park your boat in your garage or in the backyard and forget it until you're ready to go somewhere in it again. Being able to forget your boat is important. That's how you'll know it's your property, that it belongs to you, not you to it. I love sailing but I have only recently learned wisdom. My wife taught me.

...and forget about it. (Photos by C. King)

What Will It Cost?

When I was a boy, my family sailed around the Chesapeake in a big steel cutter we'd built ourselves. My father did the lion's share of the heavy work on her. One year, when we got a temporary break in the winter weather, we drove on down from Philadelphia to have a visit with it. The steel hull was immune to damage from the kind of ice Maryland's Eastern Shore usually dished out, so we had covered the boat with a canvas tarp and left her in the water. Dad had given the yard a list of odd jobs to do about the boat and, month by month through the winter, bills for this and that had been coming in. I guess it seemed

reasonable on this warm afternoon to drive down and see how things were progressing.

After a three-hour drive, my father arrived to find the tarp still tied in place and the boat untouched since October. Needless to say, he was annoyed and took the issue up with the owner of the yard, a venerable figure in my memory—designer, boatbuilder, someone I had liked. During the ensuing discussion, such things were pointed out as the realities of cash flow over the winter season and the yard's every intention to perform all the agreed-on tasks. The old gentleman finished up the discussion like this:

"Mr. Brown," he said, "boating is a very expensive hobby. If you can't keep up with it, perhaps you should consider golf or tennis or some other less expensive form of recreation."

My anger and frustration return to me fresh whenever I recall that conversation. My parents always worked hard. My father has worked relentlessly as long as I can remember, but we never were able to go sailing—or do anything else for that matter—as though we were indifferent to the cost. I was stunned by the arrogance of the man to suggest that if we couldn't go effortlessly, we shouldn't go.

For the record, we switched boatyards, smashing a gratifying path through the Choptank River ice in the process. I'd like to return, for the moment, to the yardmaster's premise: that if we can't go effortlessly, we shouldn't go. I couldn't disagree with that more profoundly. If the sea "belongs" to anyone, it is to those who love it, rich *or* poor. I'm going to assume, dear reader, that you, like me, can't go effortlessly, as though you were indifferent to the cost. So let's take a look at the cost of owning a boat. I've developed an obsession on the subject, even kept records on boat prices going back over the last two decades. You can't keep records for 20 years without noticing things; what do they show?

1. Although boats are sold on the basis of their length, you really pay for them by the pound. Obviously, a boat with expensive fittings and fine cabinetry will cost more, but basically when you buy a fiberglass boat, you're buying fiberglass by the pound. At the time of this writing in 1993, plastic yachts cost $7 a pound. In 1980, they cost $4 a pound. In 1974, 20 years ago, they cost slightly less

than $3. At first blush, this will seem to be a gross oversimplification, but if you chart out the latest prices of sailboats based on their weight, you'll see an almost linear relationship. There is one discrepancy worth noting here: The smallest sailboats, those about 20 feet and under, or those weighing less than 1,800 pounds, tend to cost more, about $8 to $9 a pound. Why? Remember that even if the boat is very small, there are still manufacturing stages that must be gone through. In terms of labor, small boats are less efficient to build than larger ones. Manufacturers would naturally rather sell a few big boats than lots of little ones— a good reason why the joys of small-boat cruising are not pitched too hard.

In the last 10 years, sailboat costs have increased approximately 50 percent. The rate of increase has averaged 12 percent a year and will most likely continue that way. There is a great temptation for manufacturers to try making their boats lighter. If they can save on fiberglass, they can still bump their prices along every year and increase their profits at the same time. It's interesting to save old brochures from manufacturers to see the pounds slipping away.

2. Here's another way you can look at it. Sailboats, on the average, tend to double in weight and in cost with every 5-foot increment in length. A 20-footer will cost twice as much as a 15-footer, a 25-footer twice as much as a 20-footer, and so on. Size is expensive. Remember: Every dollar you *don't* spend on your boat is available for something else, travel for example.

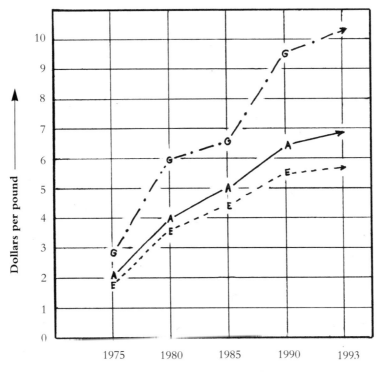

Rise in Yacht Prices Since 1975
E= economy, high-volume products...bargain boats
A= average, medium-priced for type
G= "gold-plater," fine cabinetry, custom work, etc.

The Doubling Rule of Fives

average 15–16-footer:	$6,000–$7,000
average 20–22-footer:	$12,000–$15,000
average 25–27-footer:	$24,000–$30,000

3. The cost of buying a boat is further magnified when you buy it on time. The installment plan tempts you to buy a bigger boat than you need, especially when the salesperson has every reason to pressure you into a higher ticket item. Look what happens to you when you buy on time. I made this study in 1980 and, though the brand names could stand a little updating, the point remains as sound as ever. In 1993, if you finance $10,000 over 10 years at 9 percent, you'll pay more than $5,000 in interest charges. Bank rates fluctuate all the time, but the song remains the same. Here's how the exercise went when I did it:

If you can possibly avoid buying on time, avoid it. Start very small and pay

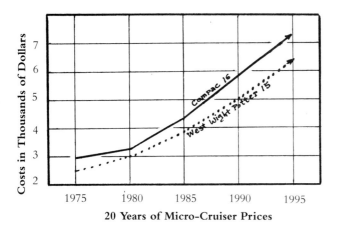

20 Years of Micro-Cruiser Prices

The ultimate object of owning a boat is not owning a boat, it's doing something in it. Think small. Pay cash. The only nice thing I can say looking back over the boats I have owned and financed is that I made enough interesting mistakes to write a book about it.

5. Let's go through an exercise to see how little it can cost to go sailing on a small boat. It's crucial to understand that fiberglass boats deteriorate very slowly. So, the well-maintained used boat and trailer you buy today for $5,000 is likely to retain a minimum of 75 percent of its value (whether bought new or used) three years from today. If that's so, then today's $5,000 boat will be worth at least $3,750 in three years. Your out-of-pocket loss in depreciation during that time will be $417 a year. Let's add to that some of the other costs of ownership and sailing:

cash. Buy a used daysailer and have fun with it for a few years while you save up. Take it places where you can camp along shore. Rig a boom tent and sleep in the cockpit, but stay out of the installment racket. How do you think the bank president affords a nice yacht?

4. The money you spend in monthly payments will end up coming out of your entertainment and/or vacation budget.

The boat	Its list price in 1980	Total including interest payments	Years of loan payments	Interest paid out	With the interest you could have bought
MacGregor 21	$5,680	$7,325	5 years	$1,660	Two windsurfers
Edel 18	$7,400	$9,500	5 years	$2,150	A Hobie 14 catamaran
Chrysler 22	$9,700	$13,900	7 years	$3,200	A 15-foot West Wight Potter
Chrysler 26	$15,300	$24,800	10 years	$9,500	A Chrysler 22
Hunter 27	$26,150	$44,500	11 years	$18,300	A Chrysler 26 (for 1 more foot!)
Hunter 30	$35,700	$63,100	12 years	$27,400	A Hunter 27

$417	Depreciation
200	Insurance
125	Maintenance
50	Registration fees
150	Gasoline to get your boat where you want to vacation
1,000	Food and supplies for two-week summer cruise
1,000	Food and supplies for two-week winter cruise
$2,942	
÷365	
$8.06 a day!	

Granted this is an oversimplification. We've neglected the costs of financing, the return you might have realized by investing money you spent on the boat, and periodic expenses to replace sails and other gear. And if you were to divide by the number of days you actually use the boat, as opposed to the number of days in a year, the daily cost would be much higher. Nevertheless, the basic truth remains: sailing need not be the exclusive domain of the rich.

Buying a Used Boat

At this writing, the market for new boats has been soft. It's a buyer's market. This is good news for people interested in buying used boats; there's enormous choice at attractive prices. It's a good idea if you're new to boating to have a boat inspected before you buy it. A local dealer, for a few bucks, may have one of his workers come down to look at a used boat with you if you're really interested.

A used boat often comes equipped with compass, anchor, line, trailer, even occasionally such exotica as a depthsounder or radio direction finder. For what you'd pay for a new boat, you can get a good used one *with trailer* and loaded with goodies. Sometimes you can produce a thick pile of folding green and offer to pay cash *right now* and get the boat for much less than the list price—especially if the seller is desperate to move it. If you're really short on money, this may be the only way to get a boat. Just keep looking and trying.

Other Costs of Ownership

Now the good news: The costs of owning and maintaining a small boat are very low. You usually can store your boat in the backyard for nothing. If you trailer your boat, you won't be leaving it in the water and can skip mooring or slip fees at a marina. Bottom paint can cost more than $60 a gallon, but you won't need any if you store your boat ashore.

Insurance on my 15-foot boat costs about $200 a year. If you plan to travel with your boat, make sure you are covered for *all* the waters you plan to sail in. It costs more to do that, but the expense is worthwhile. Imagine having an accident far from home and then discovering, upon your return, that you were not covered.

Fees go up sharply with the value of your boat. Many experienced sailors who live aboard their boats sail uninsured to escape the expense. For the best deal, contact the people who insure your car and get them to cover your boat and its trailer as well. They'll often give you a lower rate as a courtesy if they already cover your house or car. Shop around to make sure you're getting the best price.

A Sailing Expedition

You're planning for your two-week vacation. You've got the spot picked out—a big lake about 300 miles from where you live. What's this going to cost?

1. Obviously you've got gas out and back. Add 25 percent for excursions.
2. Let's assume you've got space in your boat and in your car, wagon, or van to bed down everybody in your family. Maybe you have tents, too, though you can't use them everywhere. (You can pull over at a highway rest area for the night, but you can't pitch a tent there.) If you've got a bed for everybody, then you won't have the expense of motels to worry about. Budget one night's worth, though, just in case you have a period of rain and morale gets low.
3. Rough out menus for the time you'll be gone. From that you can calculate your food budget. Find out what it costs to feed your family at McDonald's and assume you'll eat out one meal in four. I know, you've promised yourselves that this time you won't do that, but you will. It's vacation. Budget it in.
4. Add up gas, food, and lodging... then add 50 percent. "What for?" you ask. "We've been so scientific up till now."

Damned if I know. All I know is we run out of money every year and never do anything noticeably stupid. I don't know where it goes; it just goes. Take half as many clothes and twice as much money and you'll be fine. Trust me.

A Final Thought

What does sailing really cost? Look at it this way: Divide the cost of your boat per year by the days of sailing you get in. That's what it costs.

There are two ways you can improve on this picture: Spend less and sail more. If you want to do both of those things, *get a small boat*. You'll obviously spend less. Not so obvious, but equally important, you'll use the boat more. Taking off spontaneously on a breezy afternoon to a nearby river or lake will seem less intimidating, more worth doing. You'll do more daysailing. If you're driving somewhere interesting, you can drag your boat along without much bother and even use it as a trailer overnight should you decide to linger. And should a pretty lake appear along your route. . . .

One final advantage of a small boat: You'll spend less time trying to figure out what it costs when you're absolutely certain you can afford it.

Part II

Life Aboard

Basic Concerns

Now the crucial part. How can we accomplish in a small boat all the necessary life-support functions: cooking, sleeping, keeping clean, and storing clothes and gear? Before we deal with each of these, let's remember the backpackers again, the ones carrying everything they need on their backs. Think minimum. If you do, you *can* make everything fit.

Food and Cooking

We Americans are strange creatures. Before we eat almost anything, we either warm it up or cool it off. Room temperature, evidently, is a bore. That's a pity because it would be so much easier on our insides if we weren't creatures of such extremes.

If we could do without an ice chest, we would save lots of space and annoyance. Beer, soda, and water can be kept reasonably cool stored in the bilge. Dairy products, on the

With a portable galley, you can easily bring everything on the beach and cook there.

On small boats, you'll do most of your cooking in the cockpit. On really small boats, there's no other place.

other hand, especially milk, spoil rapidly if not kept cold. Milk is useful mostly for cereal in the morning. It's a hard meal to pass up because cereal is so quick and easy to fix and so filling. Try out the instant and canned varieties of milk. If cereal tastes all right that way, you've got it made. If not, you can either drop cereal from your menu or buy the smallest available cooler to keep just a half-gallon of milk cold. Solid ice, by the way, lasts much longer than cubes. On a bigger boat, try a two-icebox system. Meat and other things that don't need to be available except at mealtimes are kept in the never-opened master chest, stored someplace out of the way. Keep a small (well-rationed) second cooler for juice and other thirst-quenchers handy. This, of course, if you *must* have an icebox.

Even if you can do without ice, you probably won't want to do without a stove. A hot meal is good for morale. Many foods simply cannot be prepared without cooking.

From all the scare stories I've heard and read, I'd avoid alcohol stoves. The *un*pressurized varieties that require no pumping or priming are certainly safer, but any flammable liquid fuel stored in a small boat is a hazard.

Sterno is simple and very safe, but the flame isn't hot enough for some cooking. You may not be able to make pancakes on a sterno stove. There is a good gimbaled stove made for sterno, but it's bulky and you may not have room for it in a really small boat.

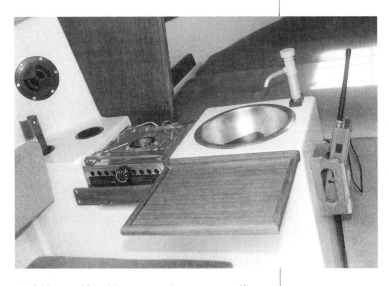

A fold-up table adds space to the compact galley of the Precision 21.

The galley of the Sunrise 24 has full headroom.

Propane camping stoves are probably the best bet. They put out a good hot flame, and some of them are very compact. We have a single-burner propane stove and a simple sterno stove as a backup for low-heat cooking—like soup. It's a good idea to have a portable galley to set up in the cockpit or to take ashore for camping.

Eggs actually keep at room temperature for quite a while. Liquid margarine in a squeeze bottle keeps nicely, too. It's good for frying or on sandwiches. Fruit, lettuce, tomatoes, onions, and carrots all keep well for a few days. Rice, dried grains, and beans, of course, are ideal.

Camping-supply stores often stock freeze-dried meals that are light and compact. Supermarkets have soup, stew, and hot cereals in freeze-dried packets. Try these out at home and see what you like.

Of course, there's always canned food. It stores well in little out-of-the-way places, it keeps, and some of it even tastes pretty good. Again, while ashore, have one "can night" a week and try things out.

Make up daily menus in advance, before you leave. Try packaging the contents of each meal in Ziploc bags and label each bag. Everything you can do at home, do at home.

Finally, try packing everything into two open, plastic laundry baskets. Check for fit under your quarterberths or wherever you have space. Put pots, pans, cutting board, dishes, mugs (which can also serve as bowls), can openers, matches, silverware, spatula, and stove in one basket, food in the other. Pack all food into plastic bags or watertight containers. Carry a plastic bag or two for trash. Now you're all set. What you've got is easy to get into and out of the car and into and out of the boat. On a bigger boat, you may eventually build in a galley, but with this system, you may not want to bother.

Sanitation

If you're in fresh water, keeping clean is usually as simple as falling overboard with a cake of biodegradable soap. If you're in salt water, you can get clean but you still have to get the salt off. Salt permeates clothes and bedding and attracts moisture. Soon everything begins to feel clammy. A solar shower is a simple way to rinse off. A stingy way to rinse off with a limited supply of fresh water is to take a sponge bath, starting at your head and working down. The cockpit floor is an ideal and semiprivate place to bathe.

Dishes can be washed in shallow plastic pans. A pan for soapy water and a pan for fresh makes sense. When you wash in cool water—especially if it's cool salt water—you need all the help you can get. Teflon pans help. For dishes as well as for you, use a biodegradable shampoo.

Finally we come to everyone's favorite, the marine toilet. Coast Guard regulations forbid toilets that discharge waste over the side. I find it strange that many yacht owners, who claim to love the sea, take such perverse pride in flouting the intent of this law. The law is worded in such a way that it is legal to go sailing with *no* toilet. Many sailors carry a sweet-smelling cedar bucket and operate on a "bucket and chuck it" philosophy. After all, it's not illegal to have a bucket that discharges over the side. Let others do as they like, sailors should be the most untiring advocates of marine ecology. We should, therefore, take care not to foul the waters we sail and swim in. I grant you, sometimes you will take your Porta-Potty ashore and empty it in a marina toilet only to flush it back, via municipal sewage pipes, to the waterway. Shame on them, then. Get the town to clean up its act. If we finally succeed in poisoning our oceans, the jig will really be up. So forget about cedar buckets and get a portable head.

On boats from 17 feet and up, there's usually a convenient spot ready-made for a marine head. On many smaller boats, especially centerboard boats, there isn't a convenient spot for the thing, and when you move into the cabin

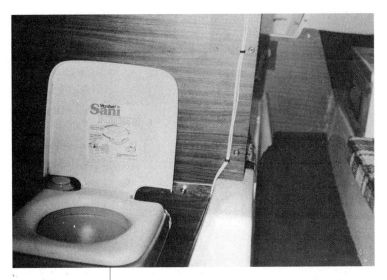

The portable toilet. Some models cost less than $70.

at night it moves out into the cockpit. You wouldn't want it next to your nose anyway.

Actually, portable heads are OK if you empty the holding tank periodically and add deodorant. The inexpensive ones have one drawback: they're flexible. When you sit on them, they squash just a bit, and when they squash, they exhale a puff of vapor from their holding tank. That's why you want to change the tank often and not allow it to ferment in your boat for a week or two between voyages. If you have space on your boat for a larger, more heavily built potty and can afford one, you'd be well advised to make the investment. On long car trips, the portable toilet can be handy if rest-stop locations are few and far between. Here also, the cedar bucket just won't do.

Sleeping

Go lie down somewhere, just to see how much room you need. Don't just lie there at attention—be natural. Now measure. Length, for some reason, is more critical than width. You need room for your feet to extend when you lie on your stomach. A narrow berth is manageable if you're wedged into it, but it's hell if you're falling off one edge all the time. Many small boats offer berths that require a filler cushion placed between them to gain a comfortable width. Sometimes flotation cushions or seabags can fill in the gap. Before you go on your first cruise, try taking a nap aboard, even while the boat's in your backyard. You'll learn a lot that way.

You've got to keep your bunks dry. That's hard on a small boat with kids in wet bathing suits crawling around. Large trash bags pulled over the after part of the cushions will shed water during the day and can be pulled off at night. Sleeping bags can be stored in heavy-duty trash bags by day if there's a chance spray or wet children will soak them.

Try inflatable camping pillows covered with regular pillowcases. Don't inflate them too much. If you like them, leave your house pillows at home. If inflatable mattresses fit in your boat, use them. They can't get soaked through and they provide additional flotation in an emergency.

Unless you have a big boat and adequate storage, don't bring sheets. On warm nights, why not sleep naked or wear light clothing? It's best to keep one set of warm sleep gear

The interior of the Com-Pac 19

separate and never ever use it for anything else. That way you're sure to have something dry when you go to bed.

So here you are, your very first night on your new boat, bobbing at anchor. You and your husband are snuggled into bed. It's cozy. You both grin. Through the open hatchway you see stars coming out. This is going to be neat. Soon your husband's regular breathing tells you he's asleep. You notice a slight pressure on your bladder and speculate idly whether you'll last the night without having to visit the head. Considering that and other imponderable questions, you drift off to sleep.

You're awakened suddenly by a loud bump. You note the wind has risen and the boat is zigging and zagging around at anchor. The sail you had carelessly furled last night has partially come loose and it's flapping restlessly. It's so warm in your sleeping bag, you decide to ignore it all and wait till morning. For some reason, however, you're suddenly attuned to each and every sound, however subtle. Somewhere in the distance, someone's dog barks. The bump returns—but only once. You glance at your husband and he's blissfully asleep! A gust of wind makes the boat tremble. Looking out the window, you realize with panic that the view is totally unlike the one you went asleep to. *By God, you're adrift!* You spring to action and are in the cockpit in a trice. It's colder than you could believe for the time of year and wet, too. Your bare feet are wet and cold. Looking around, you realize the wind has shifted. You're still in the same place, just facing a different way. Feeling your wet way carefully along the cabintop, you gather in the sail and tie it down. Your foot slips and you sit your bare fanny down on the cabin roof. The

voice of your husband comes to you through the hatch. "You all right?"

Back in your bunk, teeth chattering, feet throbbing with cold, you find your husband has taken you at your word and is again fast asleep. You settle in and, at this point, realize you won't make it to morning without returning to the cockpit to use the head. . . .

Before turning in for the night, check around the boat for things that make noise. If the halyards ping against the mast when the night breeze gets up, tie them out to the shrouds to get them away from the mast. When I was a boy, I remember being lulled to sleep by the slow, soft slap of halyards against the tall wooden masts of the vessels we used to sail. The nervous ping-ping-ping of nylon on aluminum has taken all the romance out of it.

If your centerboard is down, it may bump back and forth in its trunk. If your mast is loosely stayed, it too may thrash around. Tie your tiller amidships so it won't bump. Finally, check your anchor to reassure yourself that it's holding securely. Check your surroundings carefully so you'll be able to tell if you've drifted. There. Now you can get some sleep.

For all your best precautions, don't be discouraged if on your first night out you sleep poorly. After years of sailing, my first night on each trip is often fitful. There are sounds to get used to and my instinct is to consider each noise and satisfy my mind that I know what it represents. Then there are stars. Nights on the water, especially moonlit ones, are so beautiful that I can often lie awake hour after hour just soaking it in. I remember doing so as a boy. We have forgotten such things, living as we do, and when we find them again we are stunned, almost in disbelief.

Even if you do lose some sleep the first night out, later nights make up for it. After a few days of getting up with the sun and going down with the sun, I am sleeping with a soundness and waking with a wholeness I rarely find on land.

Stowing Your Gear

The usual weekend sailor packs everything into a cylindrical canvas seabag. This is tossed onto a bunk later on. There are two things about seabags: They take up space where someone might sit or lie down, and no matter how you pack, the thing you want is always on the bottom. The smaller your boat, the more urgent it is you do away with seabags. The secret is to hang the inside walls of your cabin with monkey hammocks and thin canvas pouches. Give everyone on board one monkey hammock and one canvas pouch. Sleeping bags can be rolled tight and tucked against the cabin sides; pillows can be stuffed out of the way in the peak. If you can keep the bunks clear for sitting or sleeping, you can cruise in comfort—even in a tiny boat.

It takes practice to get your gear down to the bare essentials. Make it a habit always to check after each trip to see what you used or wore and what you didn't. Next time leave home everything you did without. In terms

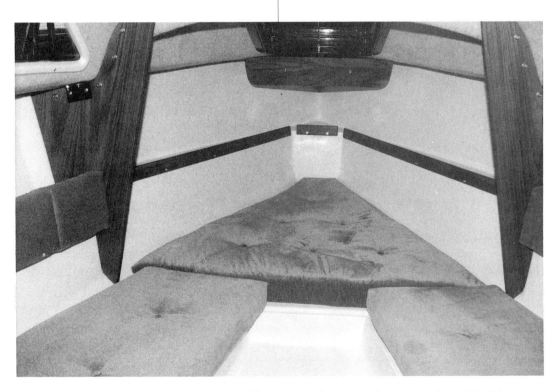

The interior of the Precision 18. Here's the challenge: How do you set this boat up for cruising? Where will you put the toilet, a stove, food supplies, your clothes, and yourselves? It's entirely possible—even on much smaller boats.

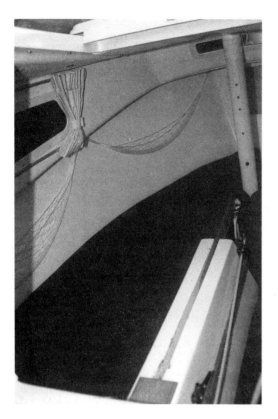

Here's the first step—a vital one—to moving in. Hang the sides of the boat with monkey hammocks, pouches, wicker baskets, whatever works. Get your stuff off the bunks and floor so you can actually crawl in and lie down if you want to.

of clothing, here's a suggested list of what to bring:

One pair of swim trunks. This will probably be your basic wardrobe. Tank suits double nicely as undergarments, since they're easy to wash and dry in a flash.

One pair of comfortable shorts. Try to keep these reasonably dry. You'll live in these.

One pair of underpants (for men). They'll feel great after your first shoreside shower before going out for a seafood feast.

One pair of comfortable long pants. These should be light color (preferably white) and of a fabric that dries quickly. In cooler weather take those pants you know you should have thrown away years ago but love too much to give up.

An old white shirt. After you've gotten sunburned, you'll wear this. Get it wet to cool it off on hot days—even jump in with it on.

Two pairs of white socks—one to wear after your feet and shins get sunburned, one civilized pair to wear ashore.

A comfortable, very loose-hooded sweatshirt. It's for sleeping. Get one two sizes too big. The loose hood can be pulled down over your eyes to keep the early morning sun from waking you up.

A really warm wool sweater. The one you're embarrassed to wear in public anymore will do fine.

A floppy hat. Get a white one. This will shade your eyes and the back of your neck. Soak the hat from time to time to keep your head cool in hot weather.

A pair of sunglasses and a pair of clip-on sunglasses. If you're sailing west at sundown you may need both at once to cut down the glare. The sun reflecting off the water, off white fiberglass decks, and off the sails can give you a headache and can even damage your eyes.

One pair of really beat-up sneakers for going wading when the bottom is rocky or strewn with broken shells or glass.

One pair of presentable sneakers to wear when the grubby pair is wet or for wearing ashore.

A knit shirt and white shorts for cutting a yachty figure ashore or for looking appealing enough to convince some seaside facility to let you tie up at its dock overnight.

A cheap $3 set of rain jacket and pants. The top doubles as a windbreaker. Discount stores sell these. Foul-weather gear is for yachts. The disposable kind folds up into a tiny pouch and takes up no space. If it's a warm rain, just wear your bathing suit.

That's about all the clothes you'll need on most summer cruises. Just remember that the ultimate purpose is to be out on the water and to see new places. I've often brought so much stuff I had little room left to turn around. I can't remember when I've been out cruising and wished I had more clothes.

Stowing Gear Outside the Cabin

Many boats have cockpit storage bins called *lazarettes*. These are marvelous for storing fenders and life jackets. If your boat doesn't have one, you can hang things on hooks from the inside of your transom. Oars can be fitted through the oarlocks and tied to the stern cleats so they won't fall out. You can drill small holes in the blades of oars to facilitate tying them down. You can also tie oars to the shrouds or figure some way to attach them to the mast. In either of those places, they may slam around while you're rocking at anchor and keep you awake.

A bow pulpit is a good idea. Not only is it a safety feature for kids, who love being up in the bow, it's a perfect perch for your anchor and line. Stern pulpits are also ideal for hanging gear out of the way, as well as welcoming things to lean up against.

Always remember that the worst place for anything is on the floor or lying on the bunks. A mess on a small boat is bad for morale and it's dangerous if anyone has to move around in a hurry.

One last suggestion. Designate certain clothes as "boat stuff" and keep them on board in the monkey hammocks. You might need to launder them when you get home, but store them all aboard. Store old pots and pans aboard, too. Then, when the mood strikes you, grab some food and go. Just like that. Knowing you can run off and go sailing whenever the mood strikes you is the greatest comfort of all.

Bringing Pets Aboard

When I was a boy, we used to sail with our Siamese cat. Of course, we were sailing a big catboat so his presence aboard was a visual pun, so to speak. It was a wooden boat, so when the cat got unnerved, he could dig his claws into the deck (or wherever he happened to be) for a foothold. I'm sure he went to the bathroom somehow, but I have forgotten the details.

Cats have been traditional crew on ships for a very long time. They catch mice, are quiet, clean, surefooted, and reasonably small. I had a seagoing cat, Magellan, a few years ago. He went riding on my first Potter and seemed to like it, initially. During our first cruise in rough weather, Magellan found he couldn't get a clawhold into fiberglass. He lost his balance while up on the cabintop and tumbled off into the cockpit. Cats have an innate sense of dignity and Magellan didn't appreciate the loss of his. He retired to the inner recesses of the cabin to think things over. That night, we tied up in Woods Hole next to a 50-foot steel fishing boat. The boat had an enormous woman aboard who made a big fuss over him. Later that night, the wind shifted and we got the full aroma of our neighbor's cargo. That must have been more temptation than Magellan could bear. By morning, the screen on the main hatch was pushed out and our cat was gone. So was the fishing boat. I imagine Magellan is rolling in ecstasy in the bilges of what must seem to him a 50-foot can of cat food. He probably weighs 30 pounds by now.

I sailed out of Woods Hole feeling abandoned and lonely. Since the morning Magellan jumped ship, I haven't taken another pet sailing, nor do I expect to.

Pets are fun, but on the water you have these problems: They fall overboard; they get stepped on; they get frightened and moan piteously, demoralizing the children.

Furthermore, pets eat and go to the bathroom, both of which, especially the latter, are real problems on a small boat. A cat's box is hell to live with in a space the size of a phone booth. If you heel way over and distribute the contents of that box into the secret recesses of your bilge, you may as well burn your boat.

Dogs are worse, making much more noise and requiring not only food but regular walks ashore. People with big powerboats (you know, the kind with flying bridges and acres of plate glass) often keep dogs. They're always poodles. I met a couple living aboard a small sailboat with their German shepherd. I remember seeing the two of them rowing ashore with this huge black dog wobbling precariously in the bow of the dinghy.

Someday, when I become rich and famous, maybe I'll have a really big boat with one stateroom just for pets. The floor will be lined with newspapers and I'll put an exhaust fan in each porthole. Until then my animals will stay ashore.

Using the Cockpit

The smaller your boat, the more vital it is to tent over your cockpit and make use of its space. If the cabin of a small boat is your boudoir, the cockpit is your living room and kitchen all rolled into one. If your boat has only two berths and if your crew consists of more than two, then you have another reason to come up with a reliable rain cover. People have to sleep out there. The first order of business is to contrive a wooden cockpit floor that can be raised level with the seats. That creates a nice double bunk.

Hatchway Tent

This is the simplest there is. It covers half the cockpit and the hatchway. You can get into and out of the cabin in the rain and have a dry spot outside the cabin for the head.

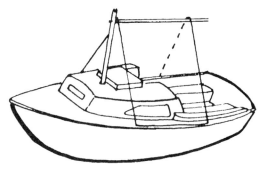

Full Cockpit Boom Tent

Obviously, you get better protection. Takes up more space to stow. Harder to get into and out of the boat. Sitting in the cockpit is cramped. Modern short booms still expose the aft cockpit to rainfall.

"Conestoga Wagon" Cover

Variations of this approach can turn your cockpit into another much bigger cabin. Sitting is dry and comfortable. The Conestoga cover is the most bulky to store, the most elaborate to set up, and offers the most windage when a squall comes up.

Boom Tents

The simplest shelter solution is to make up a boom tent. All you need is a waterproof tarp that can be draped over the boom and snapped or tied in place outside the cockpit coaming. The tent should also cover the entire hatchway and should preferably have end flaps to keep wind-driven rain out. The one drawback of boom tents is that the sides slope abruptly and leave little room to sit up in the seats. Still, they are the least-expensive and simplest option available.

A simple boom tent converts this Leeward 16, an open daysailer with a cuddy, into a snug overnighter. (Photo courtesy Luger Industries)

Bimini Tops

A more elegant and flexible system is the Bimini top. The Bimini top folds down over the cabintop when not in use, then pops up to shelter the cockpit. Most boats can be rigged to sail with the Bimini top in place. Biminis provide marvelous sun protection. You'd need side panels to keep the rain out. They tend, however, to leak or blow open in strong winds. Bimini tops also are expensive. If you have inside provisions for the whole crew, the Bimini top would be a wonderful luxury—even a necessity in southern latitudes.

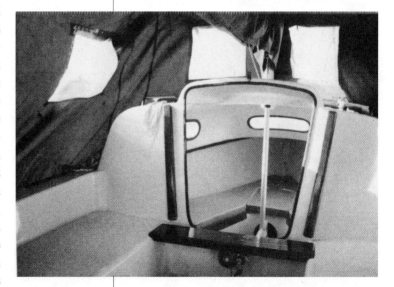

Here's going in style! The Siren 17 offers this elaborate cockpit shelter that turns the whole area into a dry, well-lighted extension of the cabin. It's not inexpensive but costs a lot less than a bigger boat. (Photo courtesy Vandestadt & McGruer)

The generous Bimini top on the Tramp trimaran

Dodgers cover only the hatchway and the after end of the cabin. They shield the cockpit from flying spray and, in rainy weather, allow you to leave the hatch open so you can get some air.

Conestoga Tops

A third option, standard on the Drascombe boats, custom-built on anything else, is a freestanding "Conestoga wagon" affair using fiberglass wands or lengths of ½-inch plastic plumbing pipe. Three of these can be bent in graceful arcs to cover the cockpit and secured to the outside of the coaming. A tarp can be draped over top and tied down. Then you can sit normally in the cockpit seats without hunching over. With part of the tarp rolled back for visibility, the boat could even be sailed or motored that way, depending on the height of the shelter.

In one form or another, you'll gain enormous benefits from weatherproofing your cockpit. The cost of the covering, even a sophisticated one, is well below the cost of a larger boat. Maybe that's the best way to look at it.

Camping Ashore

Another highly enjoyable option is to purchase a camping tent, store it under the cockpit floor, and spend an occasional night ashore.

A Conestoga cockpit cover maximizes the space on very small boats.

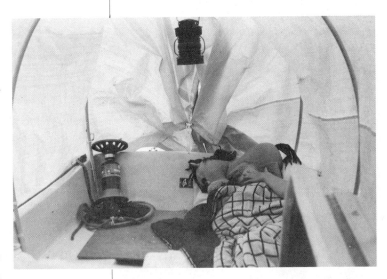

With a Conestoga cover, the enclosed cockpit is light and airy. The flexible plastic pipes stow inside the cabin when not in use.

If you own a truly beachable boat, this offers enormous flexibility. Of course, the tent is available for overland camping trips, too. Some cruising areas are too populated to allow shoreside camping, but tenting in wilderness areas is not only possible, it's delightful.

Finally, don't forget hotels. If you're near seacoast or lakeside towns, budget yourself one night in a hotel. Then if it rains when you're already wet, if you've been hot all day and at 8:30 P.M. it's still 92 degrees, or if for any reason a night of luxury appeals to you, go for it. Tie up, lock up, and enjoy a long shower and night out in a strange port.

Some Good Reading

The Big Book of Boat Canvas: A Complete Guide to Fabric Work on Boats, by Karen Lipe. International Marine, Camden, ME.

The Complete Canvasworker's Guide: How to Outfit Your Boat Using Natural or Synthetic Cloth, Second Edition, by Jim Grant. International Marine, Camden, ME

Comforting Thoughts

Being comfortable at sea consists primarily of the following:

- Being warm when it's cold
- Being cool when it's warm
- Keeping yourself and your things dry
- Keeping the bugs away

Keeping Warm

This may sound simplistic, but we'll assume that you can always put on a sweater or a windbreaker when you're cold. A candle lantern in the cabin can take the edge off a cool night without suffocating you or subjecting you to the risk of spilled kerosene from one of those nautical lanterns. You can stick a flashlight to the cabin wall with Velcro for a multipurpose light, but it sheds no warmth. Basically, as long as you can stay dry, you can probably stay warm.

Keeping Cool

Staying cool, especially in the tropics or in midsummer, is more of a problem. Most small production boats offer little ventilation, sometimes none. For moderate cost you can add air scoops to your foredeck or cabintop. They really help and, faced away from the wind, even work in the rain.

As we've already mentioned, Bimini tops give you the chance to sail in the shade. Especially if some of your family sunburn easily, this is important. The simple spray bottles sold to spray the leaves of houseplants can lay down a light cooling mist over your skin on a hot day. If you have tots on board, be careful they do not proceed, back home, to direct *other* sprays into their faces and onto their skin, expecting similar relief.

At the risk of looking like the Good Humor man, wear white. Wear thin, loose-fitting whites and spray your upper clothes with water and let the evaporation help cool you. Wearing a wet bandanna around your head helps keep the sun off and keeps your head cool. Being bald, I'm lost without one. Working on the same principle, a damp towel can help keep the ice chest cool, too. Glare from water and white fiberglass can be severe. Bring sunglasses and sun block. Frequent swim stops are good for morale, too.

If your clothes should be white in hot weather, your towels should be dark—black, brown, or navy blue. They'll dry a lot faster.

Keeping Dry

We've already discussed ways to keep your bedding dry by protecting mattresses and sleeping bags with plastic bags. While dodgers don't offer much sun protection, they shield the cockpit from flying spray and permit you to keep the hatch open while it's raining. Dodgers and Biminis offer you some of the comforts of bigger boats without the hassles and expense. Looked at that way, they're a bargain. They're much cheaper than a bigger boat.

Keeping Bugs Away

Even when everything else is perfect, bugs can ruin everything. There's a new electronic device on the market that's supposed to emit an ultra high-frequency tone that bugs can't stand. If it works, get one for your cabin (and maybe one for your cockpit if your boat is that large) and disregard all further discussions about attached screens and bug repellent. If you can't find one of these miracle devices, or if you can't afford one, or if it proves ineffective, screen kits that attach with Velcro are sold in most marine supply stores. I made up my own screens with Velcro, mosquito netting, and a sewing machine. The folded screen doesn't take up space when not in use, and you'll need it in many of the places you sail. Screening in a boom tent or Bimini top is a more expensive proposition. Still, nothing beats sitting out in the cool of evening and watching the sun go down knowing the little bastards can't get to you.

Remedies of last resort: Take a prolonged swim at dusk and don't come out till it's safe. Get a spray can of bug repellent and use it liberally. A little bug repellent sprayed around the places where your screens snap or attach to the hull or to the Bimini top will discourage bugs from crawling through the chinks in your defenses.

Trailering and Launching Your Boat

Trailering

Boats are potentially romantic objects. Trailers are not. You'll walk down the dock and look fondly over your shoulder at your boat, but you'll never walk past the parking lot and admire your empty trailer. The whole allure of trailerable boats is the promise of covering the miles at 55 miles

Ways to Go

On the Road Overnight
4 people in a medium-size boat
2 people in a small boat
*2 people in a small boat, 2 more
  in wagon, van, or tent*

On the Water Overnight
4 people in a medium-size boat
*2 people in a small boat (kids in
  cockpit)*

*2 people under boom tent in open
  cruising boat*

*2 people in cabin
2 people in tent ashore*

per hour until you get to the places you actually want to sail around in, whereupon you slip effortlessly into the water and the romance begins. Hours, days, weeks later, romance done, you haul the boat out, put it to bed, and speed home again. Such is the theory. Funny thing is, we give little thought to the one thing that makes all this possible: the trailer.

We're encouraged by most makers of small boats to give little thought to the trailer. Most manufacturers put adequate trailers under their boats, but make them the least expensive they can find. After all, it's the boat you want; you know you need a trailer, but

paying for it is an annoyance. Manufacturers know this and offer giveaway trailers as boat-show enticements. In short, the trailers under our trailerable boats are like the furnaces in our cellars—we only notice them when they break. Maybe it's time to take a longer and more loving look at the wheels under our boats.

Trailers do several things. Let's make a brief list because, just as with boats, trailer design is a compromise among several factors:

- The trailer must serve as an adequate cradle for the boat when it's not in the water. This is what trailers do 99 percent of the time.

If you can really travel with your boat, the possibilities are endless.

- The trailer must safely transport the boat overland, absorbing all the shocks that high-speed travel is heir to without jarring the boat to pieces or falling apart itself.
- The trailer must enable you to launch and retrieve the boat with minimal difficulty—even if the boat has a keel under it and sits well above the pavement.

Maybe there are other things our trailers could do for us. We can inquire into that, too. Let's look at trailers—and how to improve their usefulness—from each of these perspectives.

Cradling Your Boat

The best trailer design for cradling your boat supports the hull with long carpeted bunkboards. The bunks flex under the hull's weight and conform, at least partially, to the contours of the boat's underside. You'll get the least stress on the hull this way, and the least tendency to deform the hull's underside by supporting the boat's weight at specific points only. The fact that bunk trailers tend to be the least expensive is an extra dividend.

When storing your boat for the winter, block up the trailer by its frame to take the weight off the tires and bearings. Tires left loaded all winter develop flat spots and will give a bumpy ride come spring.

Boats with shoal keels are harder to launch because it's harder to back down far enough to float the hulls off. Trailers can be retrofitted for roller bunks that support the hull on hard rubber rollers. Instead of pushing the boat against the friction of carpeted bunks, you can *roll* the hull off. Carpeted bunks can be both wetted down to improve their slipperiness, and lubricated with dish soap and water to facili-

tate launching. If you can figure out how to launch your boat with reasonable ease, the bunk trailer is your best, and least expensive, cradle for your boat.

Structural Integrity Underway

The first thing to do is to determine the trailer's rated load and see whether your boat pushes it to the limit. Before buying a boat, ask about the model trailer the manufacturer intends to use and check its adequacy. Remember, you'll buy the boat empty, but you'll trailer it loaded up. There should be a wide margin of safety here. Tax your trailer to its limit and it might break down if you hit a severe bump or drop a wheel into a pothole at high speed.

If your trailer is bolted together, remember that vibration is your constant enemy. Begin each day with a walk around the rig and check everything, especially the connection to your vehicle. Check the lug nuts on the wheels. How's the boat doing? Are the bolts that connect the stays to the mast and hull working loose? Be paranoid; check everything—then go over the boat carefully again before raising the mast and shoving off. A trailer with a welded frame still needs checking, and the frame itself may begin to crack with fatigue. Don't go long distances on a minimal trailer.

Your boat will need to be tied down to the trailer underway so that a bump or a flat tire doesn't roll your hull onto the highway. I've run strong line through clear plastic tubing wherever friction might damage the hull. Even a wide strap can abrade a hull on a long trip, especially if your boat has hard chines or a flat bottom presenting an edge to the line. Tie a second line from your bow eye to

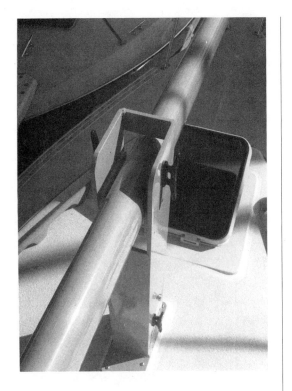

the trailer, too, so a winch failure can't result in your boat being launched off the back of your trailer at turnpike speeds. Years ago, I saw a powerboat drop to the highway somewhere near 70 miles per hour—truly a sight to remember.

Special Considerations

When towing a trailer, be a little paranoid. Something *is* following you. You can't accelerate as fast with a boat in tow, you certainly can't stop anywhere near as fast, and you can't take turns at high speeds with the same nonchalance. Drive with a timorous caution, knowing that it takes only one idiot out there to create more trouble than you can get out of with a boat in tow. Think, and drive, defensively at all times.

You'll have to be patient, too. On long upgrades, downshift and relax with some good music; on long downgrades, downshift early, ease up on the gas, and let the engine's compression ease you down the road. Repeated use of the brakes on a long downhill run might cause them to fail just when you need them most. If your load is more than 3,000 pounds, most states require surge brakes on the trailer to prevent jackknifing on hard stops. Coasting against compression activates the surge brakes. So while you're easing downhill, coast your trailer brakes. To make a long story short, you'll want a heavy tow vehicle with muscular brakes.

Boats with a heavy-duty tabernacle permit trailering with the mast in place and ready to raise. (Photo courtesy Menger Boatworks)

Launching and Retrieving Your Boat Easily

In general, the higher the boat's waterline is above the tarmac, the farther you'll have to back the boat down the launch ramp and the more difficult things will be. If you have a small, light, centerboard boat, you can expect a relatively easy time of it. Whatever disruptions centerboards make in the interiors of small boats, they pay back at the launch ramp. Let's assume, however, that you have a boat big enough to need all the help at the ramp it and you can get. What sort of help might that be?

The simplest thing you can do is order your trailer with a tongue 2 to 3 feet longer than standard. That's 2 to 3 feet additional

Burlington photographer Robert Doran happened by just in time to watch someone launch his truck. Some trailerable boats are more trailerable than others.

backing down you can do without wetting the rear wheels of your car. If you have to park your boat in a garage, though, make sure you've got room for the extra length. I've had an extended tongue on my last several boats, and it's made a real difference.

For an even more dramatic effect, adapt your trailer for a tongue extender. It fits under the frame of your trailer and slides out, locking into place 6 to 8 feet beyond the original point of connection. While your boat is still on the level, you unhook, drive ahead, slide out the extender, reconnect, and then down the ramp you go. There's only one scenario where this approach could be a problem: the ramp that comes to an abrupt end, followed by a severe drop-off. You could back down, hear a muffled bang, and see your boat drift free. But you could never reverse the procedure to get your boat out. Best go wading a little on strange ramps to check things out.

If you have a bunk trailer, install rollers on every crossbeam and lift each with an auto jack to ensure that the rollers take the lion's share of the boat's weight. The boat will

Here's an ideal launching: You back down...

give just a little push...

keep a line on the boat so it doesn't drift away...

walk it up to the shore for rigging.
(Photos by C. King)

move more easily with the bunks steadying the load, not supporting all of it.

Check also to see if your boat is nestled down as close to the road as it can get without banging into parts of the trailer or the axle. Here's where the manufacturer's mating of boat and trailer can be sometimes improved upon.

You can get a trailer with a hinge built into the tongue—usually where the tongue meets the frame. Pulling a pin releases the tilting feature and the boat can be induced to slide downhill off the trailer. Retrieving is easier, too, as the first roller the bow encounters has been dipped down below the waterline. As the boat is winched in, it climbs up onto the trailer. The heavier the boat, of course, the more strenuous the process.

Which brings us to another option: You can mount a winch with a lower reduction gear—more cranks to the foot of cable reeled in. The process will be slower, but easier. Maybe you can fit a longer crank handle on your existing winch or—for ultimate ease—mount an electric winch to do the heavy lifting.

Here's a simple modification to aid in retrieving your boat in crosswinds, when boats often blow sideways. Add a set of guide rollers to the aft end of your trailer. They flank your boat as it comes in and automatically center it as you pull it in. You can't miss.

Talk to your trailer vendor to see if your trailer could be adapted for torsion-bar suspension. A torsion-bar system suspends each wheel independently, eliminating the axle. With no axle, the load can be hung lower between the wheels, making launching much easier. RENCORP of Wisconsin made me such a trailer years ago for an experimental

Mounting a second trailer hitch on your front *fender gives you superior visibility and control for launching and retrieving. This Slipper 17 goes easily.*

shoal-draft Potter 15. It permitted the keel version to set as close to the road as the centerboard version did on a standard-axle trailer. This is an option worth looking into. There are also axles available with offset wheel mounts, permitting the load to ride 3 to 4 inches lower to the road.

Another variety of trailer substitutes carpeted bunks for roller dollies that automatically conform to the contours of your boat as it slides on. The aft set of rollers can swivel down to engage the boat at the waterline. The bow lifts up and over, and the roller dollies hoist the boat up and in, adjusting to the boat's contours continuously throughout the process. Big powerboats use this system often; sailboats could, too. You don't have the uniform support that bunks provide for long periods of storage, but launching and retrieving is much easier. Roller-dolly trailers tend to cost more than the bunk type—one reason why many sailboat manufacturers don't usually offer them as standard equipment.

Other Things Your Trailer Can Do for You

It sure would be nice if a trailer could last forever. Getting a galvanized trailer is a step in that direction. Even wheels can come galvanized. If you're a saltwater sailor, galvanizing is even more important.

It would be nice, too, if wheel bearings were immortal. Unfortunately, they require regular checking for wear. After the boat's launched, wobble the wheel from side to side, looking for play. Bearing Buddies maintain bearing grease under pressure, keeping water out. They're a good investment and are standard equipment on many trailers.

In principle, your trailer can be modified to carry more gear than just your boat. The simplest addition might be a spare wheel and tire, clamped to the trailer tongue. On long trips, this is a must. Sometimes you can get by for a short distance on a can of "fix-a-flat." You might consider carrying inner-tubes for your tires, just in case the rim gets dented and the tire no longer seals properly.

If the tongue is long enough, maybe you've got room for an ammunition box that could be clamped on to serve as a tool kit. Possibly several boxes could be fitted to carry spare parts and a jack, maybe even wheel wedges and a jack stand or two.

Heavier boats benefit from a jack stand with a wheel at the bottom that can be winched down to hold the bow after trailer and car have been disconnected. On some rigs, the bow is too heavy to lift without one of these. (For safety's sake, be sure the wheels of your trailer are blocked up before disconnecting it from the car, lest the rig take off on you.)

It's also wise to have a folding boarding ladder mounted to your transom. If you already have one, you won't need a ladder to get into your boat while on land. If a large boat requires a set ladder, design a simple holder for it when you're on the road. Some trailerable boats require the removal of the rudder. A thin plywood box clamped down under the hull holds it securely en route.

There are locking systems to foil at least casual thieves, but knowing what a big pair of bolt-cutters can do, theft-proofing is a relative thing. I don't lock my cabin while underway because any thief with a crowbar could gain entry in 10 seconds—and would destroy my hatch in the process. But then, I have a very small boat that can be easily damaged, and have little of real value aboard anyway, not even an engine.

Summary

If you're shopping for a new boat, discuss trailer options with your manufacturer in advance to see whether a trailer could be ordered specially to fit your preferences. Manufacturers might prefer not to be hassled, but it's your money and if you're willing to spend a little more, you might have an easier time launching and recovering your boat.

If you're looking at a used boat—or if you've got a boat already—consider upgrading the trailer in any of the ways described. Consider, too, if budget permits, replacing the original trailer with a roller-dolly type, or at least with a tilting trailer. If launching and retrieving your boat is a hassle, you won't go out as often; it will seem like too much work. And if you're reluctant to go, you're being cheated out of your investment, because your boat only earns its keep when you're sailing on it. It's the trailer's job to get you there safely, easily. . . and often.

To Motor or Not

At times when there's no wind (or when there's too much wind) it sure is nice to turn on some kind of motor that will get you where you're going promptly and without a lot of thrashing around. Small outboard

Many small boats row very easily. Here, the author rows his West Wight Potter.

motors are inexpensive, new or used; they adapt easily to small boats; they do the job. Why would anyone go to sea without one?

Oars

Well, for one thing, it can be fun to get around without one. It's a challenge that can be entertaining. If you were in a rush, you wouldn't be sailing, now would you? Calm can be nice. If the wind is excessive, you can reef down and get under a protected shore or run up on a beach if you're shoal draft. While you're waiting out the wind, what better time to swim, take a bath, read, make love, take a nap, organize the cabin . . . whatever. Besides, outboards smell, weigh down the stern, take up space, create a fire hazard, cost money, won't start. So to hell with them. Consider the words of Philip Bolger, author, sly naval architect, skilled boatbuilder, and innovative thinker:

> In the beginning boats were paddled and consequently had to be lowsided though they could be very long and weren't necessarily narrow. At a date not very accurately known but upwards of four thousand years ago, a genius with a blinding flash of insight made a very long paddle, set it against a fulcrum, and put the strength of his back and legs into his stroke. The next several thousand years were spent spreading the word of how well this notion worked, and refining the technique. It allowed for much heavier and bulkier vessels, though it had its drawbacks and never caught on among leads in ice, or up jungle creeks.
>
> The next brainstorm was that of using the expansion of a heated gas or vapor to turn a shaft on which paddles could be mounted, whereupon the oar went out of fashion again. It never disappeared entirely, any more than the paddle had in the age of the oar, but its use declined until few people understood its potential. A time came when hardly anybody thought a boat without expanding-gas-driven paddles was useful or even prudent. Athletes worked out in strange oar-driven machines, and children played in toys maneuvered (hardly driven) with vestigial oars, but all serious movements, such as taking the dog ashore from the moored cruiser, depended on the mechanical paddles though they, too, have their drawbacks, as follows:
>
> They're expensive, costing ten or more times as much as oars.
>
> They're complex and temperamental, needing much care and forethought to be reliable; they don't get this care and forethought and tend to stop working at inconvenient times.
>
> They need periodic refueling, and grow very heavy and bulky if designed to extend the intervals by carrying more fuel or by use of nuclear fission.
>
> They're attractive to thieves in a time in which it's unusual to do anything cruel to a thief.
>
> They're awkward and ugly objects, laborious to carry around, and they interfere with various good qualities, such as an ability to sail well.
>
> They're messy things to come near, the best of them exuding oil and grease; many of them are also noisy enough to cover sounds which, in fog or darkness, it is well to hear.
>
> —Philip C. Bolger

Outboards

Still, look around you and everywhere you see outboards. Why? Because they are convenient. Several manufacturers make really small air-cooled models that will nudge at least a micro-cruiser along nicely. An Evinrude 4-horsepower pushed my 22-foot MacGregor into almost any weather. The bigger the boat, the more sense auxiliary power makes. Remember, if you have a centerboard boat, handling will be much improved under power if you drop the board, at least partially, so that the boat can turn or pivot around it. With the board retracted, you may find steering sluggish or, if winds are strong, impossible. In my experience, an outboard is most useful in heavy winds, when you can simply drop your sails and motor in.

An outboard-motor well makes a neat installation. This system on a Drascombe Lugger offers the virtues of an inboard motor without the complexity and expense.

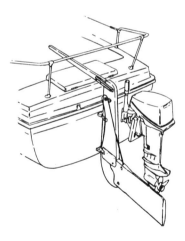

Here you see a potential problem with outboards. When the kick-up rudder is in the raised position, it can swing into contact with the outboard. Such an accident can chew up the rudder or break the shear pin on the propeller, costing you the use of your outboard, possibly at a very inopportune moment.

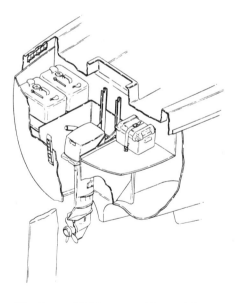

The Luger 27 kit came with an elaborate outboard-motor well system—complete with gasoline storage.

A hidden outboard is harder to steal, it's neat, clean, and leaves no unsightly clutter on your stern. It looks like an inboard, but it's less expensive and much easier to repair. (Photo courtesy Luger Manufacturing Co.)

If you use an outboard, you must reserve additional space for gasoline and you'll also need space for tools, a plug wrench at least, and spare spark plugs. Still, no doubt about it, if you have a motor, there will be times you'll wonder how anyone could possibly make do without one.

Of course you can make do. For very short distances, you can paddle. Paddles are fairly compact and store easily even on small boats. Rowing is much more efficient. You can row far longer and go much farther. Even heavy sailboats can be moved surprisingly well by the ⅙ horsepower produced by a person with oars. Stowing oars is more of a problem. You can lash them to the shrouds if they won't fit on deck. You can also check out various sizes of aluminum or plastic pipe and jury-rig collapsible oars that are lightweight and inexpensive.

Electric Motors

Another option is the electric trolling motor. Electrics are very lightweight. They start at the flick of a switch; they're silent; they don't smell; and the battery doesn't have to take up space and add weight in the cockpit. In cost per running hours, recharging is as cheap as or cheaper than gasoline. Deep-cycle rechargeable batteries are not cheap, however. You'll pay at least $100, possibly more. The battery will weigh much more than a full 3-gallon gas tank, too, though you can store it forward somewhere. New "pulse" technology offers, at somewhat higher cost for motors so equipped, up to five times more running time when the motor is run at partial throttle. By the time you've added the

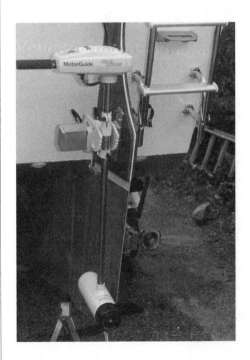

A Motor Guide electric engine powers the author's 15-foot boat silently and pollution free.

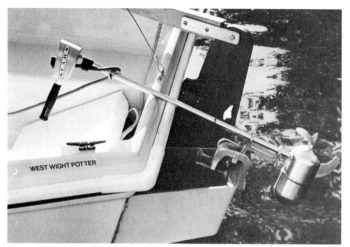

For light use, an electric motor is a convenient auxiliary. Add solar panels and you've got a pollution-free, energy-renewable closed system.

the electric motor deserves more attention than it's received.

Typical Runout Times for Three Electric Outboards at ⅔ Throttle

14-pound thrust	6 hours running time
17-pound thrust	5 hours running time
24-pound thrust	3 hours running time
"Pulsed" motor at 50-percent throttle	up to 12 hours running time

Note: 15-pound thrust approximates 1 horsepower.

cost of the battery to the cost of the motor, you could have purchased a 1.2-horsepower gas outboard. In the end, the virtues of the electric motor have more to do with reliability, simplicity, and aesthetics (no noise, smell, pollution, etc.) than anything else. As auxiliary power for at least a micro-cruiser,

What's right for you? Consider your sailing grounds. Will you be negotiating inlets or long canals? You might then need an outboard. Maybe not if are you sailing mainly on smaller lakes. Are winds fairly dependable and usually moderate? Maybe oars will be sufficient. Try going without at first. Mount some oarlocks on your boat and see. Make sure the

	Sail and Oars	Electric Outboard	Gas Outboard
Maneuvering in harbors	Good on smaller boats	Very handy	Handy
Powering while becalmed	Good for an hour or so	Good for 4–7 hours	Good
Running inlets	Difficult, often dangerous	Only the very biggest help, needs sail assist	May be the only safe and practical way
Transiting canals and rivers	Difficult, sometimes impossible, often illegal	Impractical without favorable winds	May be the only way
Running in high winds and seas	Oars not much help, rely on sail, best to stay in harbor	Not much use	Very handy

Even a 12 pound-thrust electric will move a lightweight hull.

mounting is strong. Through-bolt the oar-locks and use a backing plate. If you can get by, you've saved yourself lots of money and freed yourself from all mechanical worries. Not only that, unpowered boats in most states require no license, no numbers, no registration fees. However, if sailing seems unsatisfactory without auxiliary power, then forget what the purists say and get a motor. You're out there for fun, after all. If not, why go?

Sailing in Company with Other Boats: Why Not Get Sociable?

My coffee that first morning had the look of unrepentant Cuyahoga River effluent, gath-

ered into a glass. Instant everything, powdered creamer, forgot the sugar. Still, it was comforting to recline in the cockpit and listen to the rain patter on the boom tent. From time to time a trailer would back down and deposit another Dovekie into Edey & Duff's boat basin. This was a gathering of the clan; little *Fearless* was a guest of what was rapidly turning into a seawise and congenial collection of Dovekie sailors from all over the East.

My host, Bill Haberer, had promised me a ride on a Dovekie, and as the wind on Buzzards Bay began to pipe up, Leo and Sandy saddled up *Waterbed* and out we went. These boats can be rowed from a bench inside the cabin, so we slid out the long oars and I got a taste of the old-time galleys. The boat moved steadily into the teeth of the wind, then we raised the rig and had a boisterous sail. Leo and Sandy seemed to enjoy a continuous, scientific fiddling with the leeboards and the tiny centerboard at the bow. The Dovekie handled nicely. For a basically simple boat, there was everywhere the evidence of a thorough thinking through of all the things an owner might want to do in a small boat.

Upon our return, I was invited for another cup of coffee. For years, we've been the beneficiaries of an almost universal assumption that a boat as small as a Potter 15 must be empty of supplies. Pots were on the boil everywhere. In a comradely way, the clan was sharing vittles, booze, and stories. We departed on a half-hearted breeze to Slocum's River for a lobster feast on the beach and a morning swim over a bottom that felt like wet velvet to bare feet. Lesson one: Though privacy has its merits, sharing your experiences with an intelligent and congenial group adds another dimension to sailing.

Overnight, the sky was cleared by a northwest wind and the air almost crackled as we got underway for Cuttyhunk across the bay. I had been afraid that the other boats, 21 to 26 feet in length, would badly out-distance my little Potter, but *Fearless* held her own nicely. The lateen rig is a weatherly sail with less heeling moment than conventional rigs.

Soon we were a string of tanbark sails dotted across the bay. I could only think of some bygone time when working boats plied the coastal waters and sights like this must have been commonplace. The rousing sail was made all the richer by the company. Leo and Sandy finally steamed by and yelled, "Yahoo!"

We tacked into Cuttyhunk Harbor and eased the boats against the sandbar in shallows no other boats would have wanted or been able to use. There, we rafted up for more socializing. The food in my locker stayed put yet another day as I was invited onto a Dovekie for supper. The Dovekie's simple

interior has little furniture other than two huge storage bins that permit stuff to be casually handed in and out. The interior, which has the aesthetics of a submarine, is flexible and practical. We spent an easy night listening to the surf murmur on the bar not 50 feet away.

The clan elected to hang out at Cuttyhunk for another day. I was under more time pressure and tiptoed out on an early morning breeze toward Hyannis. The rest would continue on a leisurely two-week cruise of Martha's Vineyard and Nantucket. My father tells me that when he was a boy, yachts would rendezvous in Barnegat Bay in great rafts so that it seemed you could walk across decks from one shore to the other. Here's an aspect of sailing that remains underdeveloped in our time: providing opportunities for friendship and a greater sense of community on the water. For trailerable sailboats, the possibilities are endless: a different body of water each year.

The Dovekie clan never meant to keep this pleasure a secret; if no cruising clubs exist in your area, why not start one? If one exists, try sailing in company for a delightful change.

Sailing with Children

Someone once remarked that traveling with children is like riding third class on a Bulgarian railroad. In the best of all possible worlds, the family traveling with children has the means to do it comfortably. Usually, though, the couple with young children has not yet reached the peak of their earning potential. Money is tight and every choice is a compromise. It's usually after the kids are off on their own that a couple finally moves into a bigger yacht. Ironically, it's often far bigger than they need.

I propose that every young couple with kids be allowed to exchange their 20-foot boat for their parents' 34-footer. Then each family would have something more suited to its requirements. I know there are lots of good reasons why this idea won't work; still, there's an irony in there somewhere. One nice thing: When you sail your little boat stuffed with coolers and children and sleeping bags into a new harbor, it *is* fun to admire the floating monuments belonging to people who've made it big and then forgotten where they put it.

I digress. A book about small-boat cruising needs to talk about children because it's in small boats that you'll most often find them, since small boats are all that most young families can afford. Safety becomes even more crucial when a significant portion of your crew does not understand safety consciousness, does not obey orders quickly, and does not even fully comprehend what is going on while you're underway.

Your four biggest safety concerns with children are boredom, seasickness, carelessness, and, occasionally, fear.

Boredom

Sailing is an acquired taste. What is serene to an adult is boring to a child. Children need to *do* something. The best entertainment for kids is a secure spot in the bow. Behind a bow pulpit, kids can hang on, enjoy the motion and the spray, and ride happily for hours. Older children can be enlisted as jibsheet tenders or even taught to steer. When there's absolutely nothing to do but sit in the cockpit, you'll soon have problems. For this reason, it's best to break your day into a series of segments, stopping once in a while for a swim, a snack, beaching to explore an interesting cove, things like that. Kids like being on the water more than they like sailing—especially at first. Begin by doing things that maximize the pleasures of simply being there, gradually building the children's tolerance for longer intervals of pure sailing. Arrange to leave your kids behind with a babysitter once in a while, too. Then you can catch up on your private pleasures.

Seasickness

Seasickness is part mental, part physical. You'll notice that the people with the least to do get sick first. The bow pulpit, for all its movement, is the best guarantee against a seasick child. A few kids can play in the cabin, even in a seaway, with no ill effects. For most adults and kids, though, going below is a surefire way to feel worse. Motion sickness remedies, taken before you set out, are a good preventive measure. Some kids will get very drowsy and sleep soundly for an hour or more—sometimes longer. With my kids, sleeping off the medication doesn't seem to interfere with their normal nighttime sleep quota. It's just a natural way of dealing with discomfort. Vomiting is the other classic natural remedy for motion sickness. It often brings temporary relief. Everyone has a different tolerance for motion sickness. The best preventives seem to be things to do, medication, and occasional breaks in the routine to eat, swim, explore. There is no completely effective cure, nor will you likely be at sea long enough for a more lasting acclimatization to take place. I might also add: Don't

dwell on the issue so much as to make the condition of the children's stomachs a focal point of the trip.

Carelessness

Carelessness is a natural part of childhood. It can be aggravated by boredom and *mal de mer*. Here's where you come in, taking care to remove any sharp or raggedy cutting edges people might fall into, rigging a lifeline around a small child or a series of grab lines kids can use to get around on a deck from place to place, seeing to it that life jackets are worn, and so on. You can tell kids over and over again to be careful, but often they don't know how yet. Cause-and-effect relationships that seem obvious to you are opaque to them. In a child's life, more than in ours, things just seem to happen. This adds to their sense of wonder—and to their fears.

Fear

Sometimes, kids on a sailboat are going to get scared. They're afraid more than anything that the boat will be blown over. It's reassuring to tell them that the boat has flotation and therefore can't sink. Break off a piece of foam and throw it in the water so they can *see* it float. Act as though this is a fiendishly clever thing, this flotation. Even full of water, you can tell them, the boat will float like a cake of soap.

If you're in fresh water and have a very small unsinkable boat, you can do a swamped-canoe drill with your boat, removing cushions and contents from the cabin first. (If your electrical system is built in, forget it.) I did this with a small boat and let my wife and daughters swim around it for a while, climb in and out, and generally relax with it. If you can do it and have some way to get the water out, it's an enlightening exercise.

Kids are going to be scared by and delighted by big waves. Mostly they'll be scared at first, then the next time out they'll ask you to go where the big waves are. Your attitude is crucial. If you're relaxed and enjoying yourself, your children will rapidly regain their composure. If *you're* visibly unhinged, your family will sense that and become unhinged also.

Many children, when scared, will freeze, clinging desperately to any secure handhold, even when it's best they moved. At such a time, the lap of an unoccupied adult is best. If everyone is busy, the cabin is best. Later, make a point of explaining exactly what was going on, but meanwhile, an immobilized child is likely to get hurt. Remove the child from harm's way first.

If you sail with children, assign each one a location where he or she will be out of the way when you have to do things fast—anchor, drop sails, come about. Practice having everyone go to battle stations so that it is a reflex.

Forget "port," "starboard," "bow," and "stern" for a while. Most children are slow enough doing what you tell them anyway. "Left," "right," "up there," "back here" will

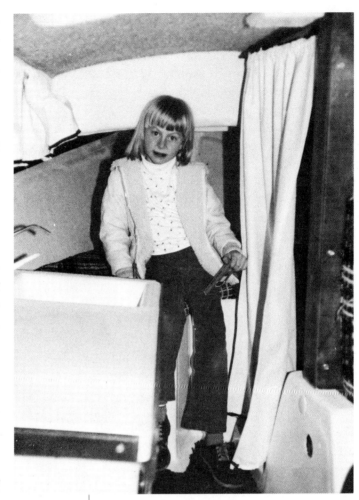

Going below in a seaway is a sure-fire guarantee for seasickness. In fair weather, though, the peak is an ideal child's haven, a cubbyhole to play in or curl up and sleep in.

do fine, and at least the kids will know what you're talking about. Many kids simply freeze when they're confused. Then you get mad and yell at them; then they decide you are hell to live with on a boat and won't want to go sailing with you.

Rehearse "man overboard" drills from

time to time. Sometimes the skipper should be the one who pretends to fall overboard and stay completely out of the action as the rest of the family attempts a rescue. Practice storm procedures too, explaining to everyone why each thing is being done.

Boredom, seasickness, carelessness, and fear are only sometime things and should not deter you from going sailing with your kids. A discussion of safety follows. It is based on the premise that one can cruise safely and enjoyably with children if the necessary precautions have been taken ahead of time.

Safety Concerns

There is no particular reason why a small boat should be considered less safe at sea than a large one. After all, when great ships are abandoned their occupants seek safety in lifeboats—and what are lifeboats but well-designed small boats? Rather than discuss what sorts of oceangoing accomplishments small boats are capable of (more on that in Part III), let's discuss instead those things a safety-conscious mariner should have in mind when setting out in a small sailing cruiser.

As the wind kicks up, this Montego 20 has its sails furled and bagged and is motoring in to safety.

Boat Flotation

Virtually all small sailing boats now manufactured in the U.S. are equipped with flotation of one sort or another—usually foam blocks. Isn't it nice to know, whatever else might happen to you, you can't sink? If the boat draws less than a foot or two and has flotation, then even in a hard fix (I'd call being capsized a hard fix) you can simply stay with your boat until it blows ashore or someone picks you up. The key is to *stay with your boat,* not exhaust yourself trying to swim to a shore that might be out of reach. Better your boat should eventually wash up on the beach than your remains. I can't be more blunt than that. *Don't remove flotation to gain additional stowage space.* How will you find words to apologize to your family while you're all treading water out in the middle of nowhere?

After all, the great virtue of these little boats is the absence of worry they offer. Keep your boat floating; keep it upright. You certainly should have a pump to remove water from the cabin. Hand pumps are quite inexpensive. Better, but more expensive, are *pumps mounted in the cockpit* that remove water from inside the boat. A bucket in the hands of a frightened sailor is also a very effective water-removal system. Big sponges are best for getting out the small stuff.

Even swamped, some boats are still capable of making headway. If your outboard weighs down the stern, unbolt it and let it sink. It's only a thing. Don't worry about it. Stay afloat. Stay upright. Even if the wind is going to pile you up on the rocks ashore, don't worry about it. It's not your life savings, and the boat—probably—is insured. Once you hit shore, you can walk out on dry land and you and your family will be safe. First things first.

You can do lots of things to add flotation. Empty plastic milk cartons add flotation and you can stuff them into odd places. Cheap inflatable swim toys can be used, too. See if inflatable mattresses can be used in place of foam ones. Figure roughly that a cubic yard of flotation will support a thousand pounds of boat and equipment.

In a Storm

Reduce sail when the wind picks up. It's less strain on the boat, less anxiety for the children, and the boat will be in better control. And, it's more comfortable. Courage and fortitude have nothing to do with it. Only a fool sails overcanvassed in a blow. Often just dropping the jib is sufficient. If you do that, pull your centerboard partway up to rebalance the boat. Better yet, reef the main and leave the jib up. The boat will handle better and, should the wind increase yet again, you can then drop the jib.

If you're anticipating a squall, run your boat up on a sandy beach until it passes. (Here's one reason why I'm partial to beachable designs in small sailing cruisers.) If you're far from shelter and have to ride it out, consider the following:

1. Get your kids comfortable in the cabin. Tell them they're in for some *real* excitement. If you tell them not to be afraid, they'll immediately start to get afraid—just as they do when you tell them something isn't going to hurt. Make them put on their life jackets.
2. Get the sails down. You may be able to use the jib, but for a real squall, it's best to have everything down and made fast.

3. You can ensure staying upright by lowering your centerboard (if you have one). You'll need your centerboard down anyway to improve your directional control under power. Tie a life jacket around the mast and run it up as high on the mast as it'll go. If you're knocked down (though almost impossible with the sails down), the life jacket will see to it that the mast cannot be rolled under. Be sure to rig a downhaul on the life jacket to get it down again when the blow is over.

4. If you have an outboard, make sure its tank is full (if it has an integral tank) and get it started. You can use it to keep your nose into the waves and to maintain steerageway. Don't pound into the waves; keep just enough throttle for directional control. Easy does it. If you only have oarpower, you can use them for the same purpose, but don't exhaust yourself. Just keep your bow into the wind.

5. Another way to keep your nose into the wind is to let out your anchor and most of its line. It will act as a drogue to slow you down as you back away, nose to the seas. Pull your rudder out so as not to strain it, or tie it off amidships. In shallow water, the anchor will take a bite and keep you from grounding. If you *want* to ground, either pull the anchor up or, if you must, let the line go with a float on the end (a milk jug or life jacket) so you can retrieve it later. Drogues or sea anchors are available, too. These are small canvas cones that create a lot of drag when trailed on a line. If you don't want to be blown to shore, these are a good investment. They stow flat and take up little space.

6. If you must, run under bare pole before the wind. Don't motor downwind at high speed; you might broach. Easy does it.

7. To sum up, whatever you may have read in various accounts of ocean voyagers caught in storms at sea, I suggest you play it safe. You're probably *not* going to be on the high seas anyway. Concentrate on keeping your boat upright and afloat, letting its natural buoyancy do the rest. Seek shelter if you can. If you can't, get the sails down, make the boat watertight, start your outboard if you have one, and ride it out. Once you realize how safe you are, you might even enjoy the excitement.

Keeping Yourself Afloat

The Coast Guard requires everyone on board your vessel to have a personal flotation device. Most people refuse to wear one. I confess, I only put one on in rough weather. Many children put up a continual fuss when made to wear one, which is a shame since they often must do so—fuss or not. It's worthwhile to take the kids to the chandlery to try on and pick a life jacket they like—even if their choice is the most expensive model. The cheap orange ones are often lumpy and uncomfortable.

It's reasonable to have a policy for each of the four "zones" on board: cabin, cockpit, foredeck, and cabintop. In the cabin, I don't think kids need jackets. Nonswimmers do need them the moment they emerge. Swimmers, in the cockpit, can sit on "throwable" life cushions, but need life jackets when they leave the cockpit. In lousy weather, wear jackets in the cockpit as well as forward.

For nighttime sailing, some form of

waterproof light and a plastic police whistle should be pinned to each life jacket, and kids should wear the jackets whenever they're out of the cabin. In any kind of "weather," so should the adults.

If you're an adult and you can't stand life jackets, an inflatable pillow, folded flat and stuffed into a back pocket, would be a nice margin of safety if you fall overboard. You could quickly blow it up and stuff it under your shirt. Buoyant windbreaker jackets are on the market now, too. Flotation need not be uncomfortable and is always a vital margin of safety.

Safety harnesses are a good investment and pad-eyes properly reinforced can be added when needed. Watch your kids move about the boat and figure out where they should be able to clip themselves on. At night, harnesses are a must as well as the small, waterproof lights that clip onto life jackets.

How to Avoid Falling Overboard

- Stay seated most of the time.
- Have lots of firm handholds. Be able to go from handhold to handhold, bow to cockpit. Teach your children (and your guests) how to move safely on the boat—in a wrestler's crouch always holding onto something, not striding around like someone walking across a living room.
- A bow pulpit is a worthwhile investment, especially for kids, who love being up there.

Protect your children. Get them comfortable life jackets they'll wear without complaint.

- Lifelines on raised stanchions can trip you up on a very small boat. Deck construction on many small boats is such that stanchions might tear out should a full-grown adult fall into one with real force. Better security is to add some extra grabrails to the cabintop. Lifelines from a stern pulpit to the aft cabin wall, enclosing the cockpit, are a fine idea—especially if you have children aboard.
- Trunk cabins are better than flush decks on small boats. Flush decks, when wet and the boat is heeled over, become slick sliding boards. You can sit on a cabintop and inch your way along.
- Get white bathing suits for young children. My father-in-law insisted that all his children wear white bathing suits while they

learned to swim. White suits are much easier to spot underwater. During family summers on Buzzards Bay, the kids lived in the water. Because of the highly visible suits, he claims, two drownings were averted.

- Pay attention to what's going on. This is a habit that takes time to cultivate. It's good training for kids.

"Man Overboard!"

Practice throwing a life jacket over the side and sailing back to get it. Try that on all points of sail. Direct someone to do nothing but keep the "swimmer" in view at all times. Life jackets should have plastic police whistles pinned to them and, at night, small clip-on flashlights.

The *moment* someone goes over the side, throw over a flotation cushion. If a child goes over, an adult should go over, too, to lend aid and encouragement.

The person who bought the boat should *not* be the only person who knows how to sail it. See to that.

When all's said and done, it's faster to start the outboard, let the sails flap (or drop them), and *carefully* motor back to pick up the swimmer.

Getting Back on Board

Now you've gone and done it. You've fallen overboard. Or maybe you went for a swim but didn't plan in advance how to get back aboard. You swim up, drape your arm over the gunwale, and . . . and what? You're treading water; nothing to push off of there. Clearly this is going to be a gymnastic challenge. How strong are you? Can *all* members of the family muscle themselves back up?

Can your kids even reach the gunwale? Planning is required before anyone goes over the side, whether by hook or by crook. What to do?

The best solution is to mount a folding ladder on the transom. Now *everybody* can get on board. Be sure to back up any through-hull fittings with oversize washers or, better yet, large plywood pads backed by washers. (While you're at it, back up all your cleats, too. Manufacturers often scrimp here.)

If a ladder is too costly, a loop of line hooked over a cleat on the cockpit coaming can give you something to hook your foot into for a leg-up into the boat. Make sure the cleat and the fiberglass there are properly supported to take that kind of strain. If need be, add a well-reinforced fitting that will hold a boarding loop. Passing the line through a 6-inch length of heavy garden hose will provide a more comfortable purchase for your foot. In most small boats, the loop is sufficient. A rope ladder is good, but it takes up more room.

Investigate mounting a step on your rudder—on the side *opposite* your outboard mount. You might mount a rope loop from the bottom gudgeon of your rudder for an emergency foothold.

As in most things, answers are not hard to come by if you ask the questions in time.

This might be a good time to discuss swimming children. You'll get a lot of peace of mind if your kids wear some form of flotation—if only a single "water muscle"—while they're swimming. You might ask them to swim off the stern where you can see them. Children tend to be lost from view as they swim around to the bow.

If you're riding at anchor, you'll notice

that most small boats tend to "sail" around a lot, wander back and forth on their lines. A very young and weak swimmer could be pushed under the boat as it started its gradual swing in the opposite direction. This risk should be explained clearly to little children, and they should be confined to where you can see them. They can hold onto lines with loops or fat knots at the end. You can festoon the boat with such lines if your children are very young. Mooring lines are perfect. Dangle one from the bow, one from each of the stays, and one from each of the stern cleats. Before the children go in, you should check the water. Currents, even small ones, can be tough to see and even tougher to swim against, especially for small children. In any current, a life jacket and line are necessary. Most kids love the water. They'll probably much prefer swimming to sailing. It pays to establish safety procedures right away.

If You Do Capsize

One must begin a discussion about capsizing by stating at the outset that of course we're all good sailors here, and so naturally *we're* not about to capsize our boats. But *somebody* might do it—any time at all, really—so it's a good thing for their sakes to discuss it here.

After years of sailing, I had never come close to capsizing. I've been in all kinds of conditions in my Potters, but the little boats have a formidable reputation. In that spirit, I rushed the season and went sailing one March. The sun was strong and, after a long winter, Nantucket Sound was irresistible. While running downwind, a gust gathered strength until I was surfing a bit. This was fun and the boat was in full control. Then the boom began to lift. I veered off, but the wind veered with me and *Fearless* slowly rolled over on her side.

The cockpit of this Sirius 20 is well protected with a stern pulpit and lifelines. Note the boarding ladder on the transom.

The boom, now vertical, continued to drive the boat over. Water poured into the open companionway as I slid into 40-degree water. I had multiple layers of clothing on, a bulky sweater, and a coat. No life jacket. Had this affair cost me my life, my wife would have been justifiably furious at my stupidity.

At this point, I was unaware of the cold and had tremendous energy. I splashed over to the centerboard and climbed onto it, weighting the boat. The cabin was awash with mattresses, sections of the toilet, decomposing toilet paper, boxes and bottles, and wooden locker lids but no sign of the pump. It had washed out and away. I went back overboard to retrieve an oar, then I dropped the sail and rowed to a nearby beach. (I'd be dead, else.) By then, my teeth were chattering as I sat up to my fanny in ice water. In the end, I required a tow and some recuperation in bed. When I got home, I plunged into the bathroom for a steaming shower only to find my daughters had beaten me to it and exhausted the hot water. We all have days like this, sometimes.

OK, fine; so I've shared a potential horror story with you that turned out all right. What's in it for you? Advice is in it for you, starting with:

- Please assume, if you're in a small boat, that *you can be capsized.* Continuous awareness of the possibility is your greatest single defense. So far, every small cruising boat capsize I've heard of has taken place *on a downhill run.* Many small boats can carry more sail going upwind than down. They pound away safely upwind, then, as they turn to run downwind, they suddenly find themselves out of control.

- So *reef early.* It's easier and safer to do it at the dock, but work out reefing procedures and practice them so you won't have to perfect your technique when you're getting blown around and may be scared.

- When conditions give you cause for concern, *close your hatches!* This operation and reefing go together; when you think of one, do both. You can survive a knockdown in good order if your cabin doesn't fill with water.

- Invest in a *real high-volume pump.* Your boat could hold more than 100 gallons of water. I now have a massive pump more than 5 feet long slung inside the cockpit coaming that can evacuate a boatload of water in under 40 minutes.

- *Install a small drain in the transom* that can allow your boat to empty. In tidal waters, you can beach the boat, wait for the tide to fall, then let your boat drain itself. It's also handy for cleaning the interior while the boat's on its trailer. Remove all mattresses and perishables and hose it right down. *Always check the drain before launching.*

- *Do not remove flotation!* If your boat has none, consider adding some. You can bring along an inflatable beach toy or two to inflate in the cabin if an approaching storm makes you really nervous. Re-think your cavalier approach to life jackets.

- If you do capsize and water enters your cabin, your foam mattresses will take up an enormous volume of water. Why not replace them with *closed-celled foam that floats?* Backpackers use it all the time. Fastened to the bunks with Velcro, the stuff can help float your boat. It's more flexible than conventional foam; part of the mattress can be rolled to form a backrest.

- If you store related items of first aid,

hygiene, emergency, tools, etc. in sealable plastic containers, you'll be less demoralized if you get swamped. Paper towels, and especially toilet paper, will shred and drift around to clog bilge pumps. Cardboard food boxes will also dissolve, discharging their contents. Seal those things in Ziploc bags.

- You might not want to do this, but you can clean out your boat and trailer it to a freshwater pond for an actual capsize drill. Practice getting on the centerboard or keel, if it's needed to right the boat. How much freeboard is left when you're swamped? Can you pump the boat out while swamped? Can you row it that way? Can you move about without the boat rolling over again?

I had my education when I least expected it. It's not the boat's fault (I've seen

Reef early in high winds; speed stays good—and it's safe.

automobiles turned upside down), and when it happened, the surprise almost killed me. I hope you'll not be as complacent as I was and that you'll heed precautions.

Fire on Board

Many small boats don't have forward hatches. The only way into (and out of) the cabin is through the main hatch. Don't cook with your stove blocking the way out. A fire could trap someone in the cabin. It's best to cook outside in the cockpit, away from the outboard motor and its gas tank. A marine hibachi can be clipped onto a bow or stern pulpit and will keep the cooking completely outboard. In rainy weather, if you're confined to the cabin, you may need to warm something up. Be mindful not to block your exit. Have a place to safely set down hot pans, which will burn or melt fabric and badly scar fiberglass. A plywood strip stored under a bed cushion is ideal. Make it big enough to support both stove and two pans. Things are less apt to be overturned that way and you can move the whole operation topside when the weather clears.

Mount a fire extinguisher on a bulkhead where you can get at it quickly, even from the cockpit.

Summary

Don't let this chapter scare you or dissuade you from sailing. The difference between an adventure and a crisis is that the former challenge was anticipated and prepared for while the latter was not. With children aboard, it's even more crucial to remain composed and deliberate in your actions. Radiate confidence born out of good planning and careful preparation.

Part III

Boat Basics

The Hull

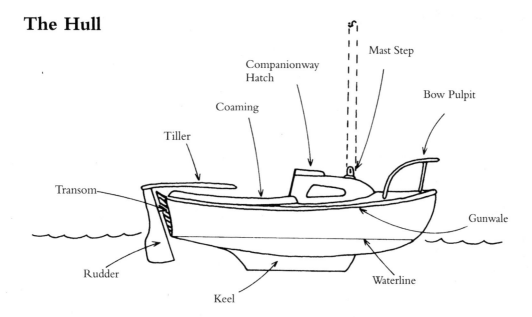

Some Nautical Terms

Draft

The maximum depth of a boat from the waterline to the bottom of the keel or centerboard.

Freeboard

The height of the hull from the gunwale to the waterline.

Beam

The maximum width of a boat.

L.O.A.

Length over all. The boat's maximum length.

L.O.D.

Length on deck; not counting bowsprits, for example.

L.W.L.

Length on the waterline. This measurement says a lot about how fast a boat will be.

Displacement

What a boat weighs.

Ballast

Weight added, usually in the keel, to help a boat stay upright.

Gunwale

The upper edge of the hull... where the hull and deck meet.

Transom

The flat after end of a boat. Canoe-shaped hulls have no transom.

Coaming

A raised edge around the cockpit that keeps water out and serves also as a back-rest. High coamings mean comfort.

Pulpit

An elevated railing, usually in the bow.

Bilge

The area under the floor of the cabin. Loose water tends to collect there and turn foul, hence the old sailor's derisive curse, "Bilgewater!"

The Basic Hull

In the simplest terms, the hull is what keeps the water out and what keeps you in. Its shape, especially its shape below the waterline, has a profound effect on the performance and liveability of your vessel.

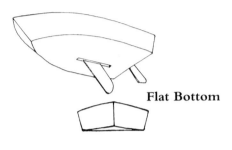

Flat Bottom

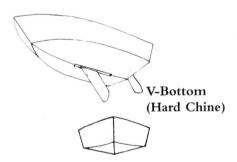

V-Bottom (Hard Chine)

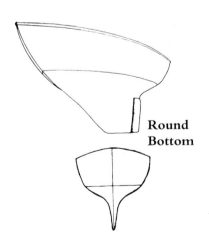

Round Bottom

The Flat-Bottomed Hull

Let's start with the simplest hull shape and consider its strengths and virtues. The flat-bottomed hull—like a rowboat hull—is about as simple as you can get. A narrow flat-bottomed hull can be quite fast under sail; a wider hull will be slower but will have enormous stability. The flat-bottomed boat will draw only a few inches, making it ideal for fishing or just snooping around over tidal flats and other shallow places where most boats can't go.

In choppy water, especially at higher speeds, the flat-bottomed hull will pound the fillings right out of your teeth. The hull takes an awful beating, too. Without a lot of power, a broad hull will be beaten back by each wave it encounters. It's not a blue-water hull. A flat-bottomed hull under sail would be blown sideways; it has so little "bite" on the water. A centerboard is the most common solution for that.

Finally, if you mount a cabin on a flat-bottomed boat, you'll find very little headroom in there. Still, there are appealing features to the simple flat-bottomed boat, and a number of commercial offerings, mostly open boats, feature flat-bottomed, shallow-draft hulls.

The V-Bottomed Hull

There's a fairly simple solution to reduce the pounding and improve the rough-water performance of the flat-bottomed hull without losing much of that wonderful stability. It's called a *V-bottom*. This shape is still very simple to fabricate, and it's used in thousands of lightweight aluminum skiffs as well as in many do-it-yourself plywood designs.

Here's the great appeal of the extremely shallow-draft boat. The Marsh Hen is sitting happily in ankle-deep water making it, and boats like it, ideal for exploring and shoreside camping. (Photo by Florida Bay Boat Co.)

The V is fairly sharp in the bow, helping the boat part the waves as it moves into a chop. Then the V flattens out aft, offering a nearly flat bottom in the stern, where the cockpit is, where people are most apt to sit and move around. This type of hull is also called a *hard-chined* hull, referring to the hard edge partway up the hull where the sides and the V-bottom meet.

V-bottomed boats can be quite seaworthy. They have good stability and tend to heel very little, preferring to sail on their bottoms. In a small boat, the V is probably the best shape.

Round Hulls

The final option is the round hull. It's deeper, can't plane or surf down waves the way the flat- or V-bottom can, nor is it apt to find its way into very shallow water without running aground. On the other hand, the deep hull offers a very comfortable ride in heavy seas and has lots of headroom and storage below. With its ballast weight down deep, the round hull will heel easily at first, then become progressively stiffer. Whereas a flat-bottomed boat can, if somehow flipped, be stable upside down, the deep keel boat cannot. It has "ultimate" stability. That makes it the top choice for deep-water sailors.

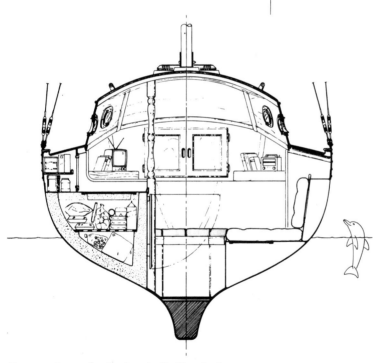

For seagoing craft, the deep hull offers the best ride, the best ultimate stability, and the greatest volume for storage. This boat, the 20-foot Flicka, can carry well over a ton of supplies for extended cruising.

Few small boats offer the full keel. Cape Cod Shipbuilding offers an 18-footer called the Goldeneye. It's been sailed across the Atlantic. Cape Dory built the 19-foot Typhoon. Both boats have bunks for four inside. To my mind, I prefer beachability and portability in a small boat, but both of these full-keelers evolved in Buzzards Bay (where there's often a nasty chop), and most of their owners moor the boats out all season and sail them everywhere much larger yachts go. For these applications, they're perfect.

Any boat that's going to sail to windward has to have some system to keep it from being pushed side-

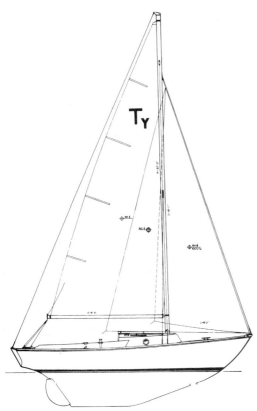

The Cape Dory Typhoon offers a full keel in a 19-foot hull.

ways by the wind and waves. The full-keel boat has no such problem; shallow-draft boats, however, have to come up with something. Let's look at the various possible approaches to solving the slippage problem.

Under the Waterline

Leeboards

The Dutch solved the problem, after the Renaissance, by adding *leeboards* to their shallow-draft vessels. These could be lowered underwater while tacking to provide some lateral resistance. The *shallop*, a small open boat with leeboards and a spritsail carried on the *Mayflower,* was used by the Pilgrims to explore the New England coast. The system is still in use in a few modern vessels. Leeboards have several virtues. They are inexpensive and simple to install. They leave the interior of the boat free of trunks, pulleys, and winches. On a small boat, this is a special blessing. The bottom of the hull is smooth and flat for easy beaching. On the negative side, most people think leeboards look strange; consequently, only a courageous manufacturer will build boats so equipped. Leeboards are usually light and thus offer no ballast advantage when lowered. Still, for very small boats, leeboards are underutilized considering all their advantages.

Centerboards

The centerboard gained great popularity in colonial times and has remained popular ever since. Housed in a trunk along the boat's centerline, the board swivels up and out of the way when beaching or when not in use. The board can be weighted to add stability. The so-called *swing keel* is simply a very heavy winglike centerboard that contributes enormous stability at the expense of imposing corresponding strains on the centerboard trunk. Centerboards require some system of pulleys or winches to get them up and down. They also intrude on the cabin space, dividing the cabin in half on smaller boats. Accommodations on larger boats can be designed around the trunk. Smaller boats are simply stuck with it. In very small boats, the central location of the centerboard trunk makes it hard to find a good location for the marine toilet—a further inconvenience. Although a centerboard boat beaches easily, one also must be careful that the trunk doesn't get packed with sand and shells, for then you'll shove off and find you can't get your board down. It's advisable to carry a small saw aboard to slip between the board and the trunk to get the sand out.

All told, despite its occasional inconveniences, centerboard variations dominate the small-boat market because they're familiar and because they usually perform well.

Daggerboards

Whereas the centerboard swivels up and down around a pin, the daggerboard simply drops straight down into its trunk sheath. The daggerboard trunk takes up less space and, if it's lightweight, the board can simply be raised and lowered by hand. On heavy boards, a winch is needed. Several modern designs use the daggerboard as a *drop keel*. The boat can be launched from a trailer, then the heavy keel is lowered in place and left there until it's time to take the boat out again. Now it's a keel boat; now it isn't.

A beachable boat like this Spindrift is ideal for exploring and camping.

Under the Waterline

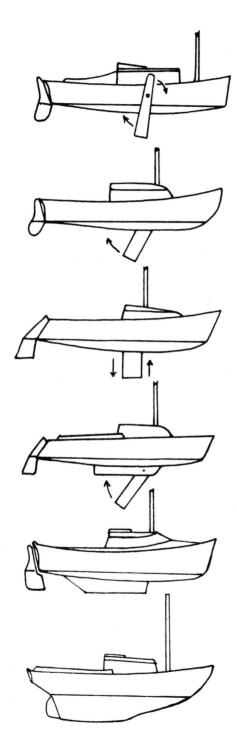

Leeboards

Unconventional, may be vulnerable to damage. Simple. Inexpensive. Do not intrude into cabin. Beachable.

Centerboard (Swing Keel)

Widely used. Also offers shallow draft. Weighted, can offer stability. Intrudes into cabin space.

Daggerboard or Drop Keel

Will not kick up if grounded. Less drag underway—faster. Simpler in a small boat. Can add stability. Intrusive.

Keel/Centerboard

Keel adds stability; board is light and is easily handled. Reasonably shallow draft. No intrusions into cabin.

Shallow (Skeg) Keel

Simple. No intrusions into cabin space. Cannot be beached easily (twin keels can). Harder to ramp launch.

Full Keel

Still preferred for ocean cruising. Deep hull—good for storage. Impossible to beach; very hard to ramp launch.

There are drawbacks to the daggerboard concept in heavier boats. If the boat strikes something on the bottom at speed, the board can't kick up out of the way as a centerboard can. All the impact will be absorbed by the daggerboard trunk. Neither can a sailor modify the underwater shape of his boat by partially raising the board to move the center of resistance aft, as he can with a centerboard. Despite these objections, a number of very high-performance boats have been introduced with daggerboards and they're selling well.

Keels

The Vikings seem to have been the first shipwrights to have put any kind of fin keel under their boats. Their vessels had shallow, full-length keels. Coupled with their advanced sailing techniques, Viking ships could make progress to windward. Several modern designs, notably the English series of Drascombe boats, still use variants of this ancient system.

Keels offer a strong backbone for the boat and great simplicity. No winches, no kick-up rudders, and no trunk poking up into the cabin interior. Keels don't permit you to actually beach your boat, nor do they kick up when you run aground. When you're stuck, you're stuck, though usually not for long.

Shoal Keels

Many small boats these days feature shallow *skeg* keels. With airfoil shapes, these keels provide effective, if not astounding, windward ability and reasonably shallow draft—often as little as 2 feet. Such designs offer many of the virtues of both centerboard and keel designs, and are gaining market acceptance.

Full Keels

For ultimate performance against the wind, a deep keel is best. Twelve-meter sloops have deep keels; most ocean voyagers do, too. You get good ultimate stability with that weight down there and can carry more sail because of it. For small boats, though, beaching is out of the question. For getting ashore you might even need a dinghy, which would be silly in a small boat. On the other hand, maybe you can moor your boat somewhere and will be in deep water most of the time. Then you'll appreciate the full-keel boat's ability to bash to windward.

Twin Keels

Several British designs solve the falling tide problem by putting two keels under their boats so they can take to the bottom easily. They gain this advantage, though, by paying a performance penalty in increased drag.

Bilge Keels

Another solution to the grounding problem is to start with a very shallow long keel and add two small additional fins where the twin keels might have been placed on a different vessel. The area of all three fins adds up to the area of one big one, and you've got a shallow boat that sits level on the beach. Windward performance is acceptable but not exceptional. This approach is a very appealing one for small sailboats: the deep cabin of a keel boat, the very shallow draft of a centerboarder... almost perfect!

Keel/Centerboard Designs

A final compromise is to house a thin centerboard inside a shoal keel. This provides for shallow draft, good windward performance, and no intrusions into the cabin interior. The

This deep-keeled Goldeneye 18 by Cape Cod Shipbuilding has been successfully sailed across the Atlantic. Small can still be seaworthy.

The bilge keels on this Drascombe Skaffie prevent leeway and permit level beaching when the tide runs out.

small boating at its best. But our applications are not everyone's. Other designs offer other virtues.

Most importantly, try to anticipate what kind of sailing you want to do and select the best hull design for that purpose. Fortunately, there is an enormous range of choices available in every size boat you might want. Small boats are so inexpensive you might consider buying two different ones so you don't have to compromise if you want a boat to sail to Catalina but your spouse's passion is looking for shells!

system is relatively expensive to manufacture and won't beach perfectly level, but it's the most recent approach to obtaining the best of both worlds.

Summary

Perhaps even more than sail shape, hull shape will determine what kind of sailing you're going to do and what the interior of your boat is going to look like. Personally, I like an extremely shallow draft in a small boat. Any beach can be a port in a storm. And I expect to trailer my boat a lot and haul it in and out of the water frequently. We also like to pull up on a deserted beach to explore, picnic, or camp overnight. This seems to be

Sailing Rigs

Many excellent texts are available on how to sail—a subject beyond the scope of this book. Some of the best or newest of these titles are listed in Appendix 5. Of major concern in this book are the different kinds of sailing rigs in use today and the advantages and disadvantages they pose to the small-boat sailor.

There are several vantage points from which we can examine any sail plan: cost, performance, ease of handling, and the ease with which we can add sail in light wind or reduce it in heavy weather. Any rig is a compromise; only you can decide which factors are most critical for the kind of sailing you propose to do.

Some Sailing Terms

Getting in irons or in stays
Sometimes while tacking, a boat rounds up into the wind too slowly and comes to a standstill, nose to the wind, sails flapping mightily. A boat is usually quite happy to stay in this position, so getting out of stays sometimes takes some effort.

Tacking

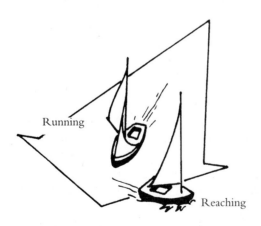

Running

Reaching

Jibing
Jibing is zigging and zagging while running downwind. Instead of coming about *into the wind, the wind suddenly catches on the opposite side of the sail and hurls it across the cockpit—often with great force. This move must be done with great care. Accidental jibes can capsize a small boat, damage rigging, or even hurt someone.*

Broaching to
This is a problem that occasionally pops up while running downwind in very rough seas. A large wave can push the stern around, throwing the boat sideways and possibly causing a capsize. Broaching and being pooped *(having a wave break over the stern) signal that it's time to* heave to *(ride it out with reduced sails up) or* lie ahull *(ride it out with sails down).*

Reefing
Reefing is the prudent act of reducing sail when the wind gets up—by tying off a panel of sail or by rolling part of it around the boom or the mast.

Tacking
Tacking, pointing, and beating are all terms for zigging and zagging upwind. Most boats can point within 45 degrees of the wind; some do better.

Reaching
Reaching is sailing at angles up to 90 degrees across the wind. Most boats are faster doing this.

Running downwind
Running downwind is drier and more comfortable, but often entails great strains on the rig and requires great concentration at the tiller.

Sailing Rigs

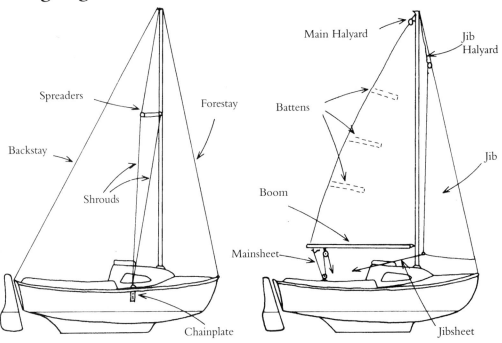

Stays or Shrouds

Fixed lines, usually wire, that keep the mast standing and distribute the strains of sail pressure to the hull.

Halyards

Lines used to raise and lower the sails.

Sheets

Lines used to pull in and let out the mainsail and jib.

Battens

Fiberglass or wooden strips used to stiffen sails and reduce flapping.

Masts

Poles used to hold the sails up.

Booms

Horizontal poles used to extend sails out away from the mast.

Sprits

Poles, often hung diagonally from the mast, that can be tensioned with a block and tackle, to adjust the shape of the sail.

The Cat Rig

If I could design my own small getaway cruiser—especially if it were light and under 17 feet long—it would have one unstayed aluminum mast, which just plugged into the deck at the bow, and only one sail. The sail would be a modern triangular design. Such a rig would be light, inexpensive, efficient to windward, and easy to set up and take down.

A traditional catboat, built by Cape Cod Shipbuilding of Wareham, Massachusetts

Single-sailed rigs, called *catboats*, have been around for a long time. The traditional catboats were working craft—heavy, broad beamed, massively built, with shallow centerboards and boom-and-gaff sails. Modern sloops point higher and go faster, but then, as Garry Hoyt has recently shown with his Freedom designs, so will a modern catboat.

There's a possible drawback that could affect some small cat-rigged boats. On most catboats, either the mast or a mast support is going to come through the cabin—usually through the foot of the V-berth. This intrusion might block off precious footroom in berths usually cramped anyway, and it might divide the bunk in half, making overnighting a somewhat less romantic experience.

Various objections notwithstanding, the cat rig offers good sailing and enormous advantages in cost, simplicity, and ease of setup and stowage. I'd love to see some manufacturers offer an unstayed cat rig as an option.

The Freedom 21, a modern fully battened cat rig enjoying a 40-knot breeze

The Sloop Rig

Most sailboats, even small ones, are *sloop rigged*, which is to say that the mast is mounted farther aft than it is on a catboat, and that a second sail, or *jib*, is hung from the forestay. On such a rig, the supporting network of stays can become complex. Most 22-foot boats will usually have a forestay, a backstay, and two stays (or *shrouds*) per side (an upper and a lower). Smaller boats can get away with as few as three stays. New boats are usually given a sloop rig for market appeal alone. It does have its virtues.

Reducing sail on a sloop is a fairly straightforward procedure. Many small boats sail acceptably well on their mainsail alone and so, in heavy wind, one can simply drop the jib.

A reefed main and jib make a more balanced rig. Some small boats can take down both sails and sail on their genoa, if they have one, at this point. Larger boats often have storm jibs to fly with reefed mains—or they have reef points on their jibs. In such wind conditions, you had best be in harbor. A reefed main and no jib will give you some control in most boats. At some point, you will have taken in so much sail that the pressure of the wind on the

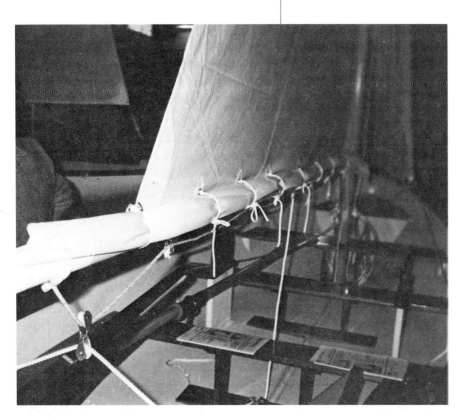

Tying in a reef reduces sail area in high winds.

hull, cabin, and rigging will begin to over-power what little sail you have left and you will no longer be able to make any progress against the wind. Small boats will gener-ally reach this point sooner than large ones. At that point, it wouldn't matter what kind of rig you're using. Short of this, the sloop has a lot of flexibility, giving you lots of options.

The sloop has a few drawbacks, however. It is more complex than an unstayed modern cat rig, there are more lines to foul up, more can go wrong. Two lines are required to con-trol the jib, one on each side of the boat. One of the crew must watch for that every time you come about.

The jibsheets should be folded in half, then threaded through the clew of the jib.

The Cutter Rig

Imagine a standard sloop-rigged sailboat. Add a second jib out there (a *flying jib*, as it's called) and you have a *cutter*. The cutter has some virtues. The staysail plus the regular jib have about the same effect as a genoa. In moderate air, you take down one of the jibs (or roller furl it); in light air, you put it up. On tradi-tional cutters, the mast is stepped farther aft, offering more balanced sail combinations. Many circumnavigators prefer cutter rigs for this reason.

In really small boats, despite the salty appearance, I think the cutter adds more complexity than it's worth. You have more stays, more sheets, more halyards, and three sails to keep trimmed and drawing.

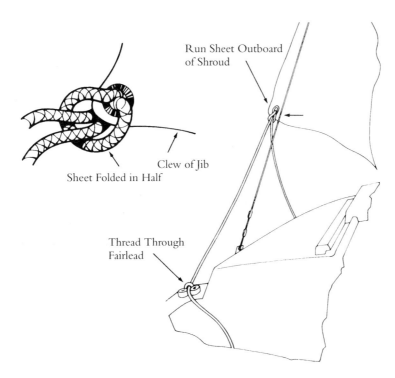

Run Sheet Outboard of Shroud

Clew of Jib

Sheet Folded in Half

Thread Through Fairlead

(Illustration courtesy Com-Pac Yachts)

More Than One Mast?

With the exception of the *cat ketch* rig (two unstayed masts, one self-tending sail apiece), what I've said of the cutter rig applies here as well. If the object is to make a miniature of some favorite old-timer, fine. If the object is simplicity of installation and operation coupled with low cost and reliability, you want to eliminate every stick, wire, line, and cleat you can. Keep it simple.

Small-Boat Rigs

Catboat
cheapest
simplest
reasonably efficient
easy to handle
preferred for boats 17
feet and under; new
concepts work on
even bigger boats

Sloop
reasonable cost
reasonably simple
more versatile
most efficient
fairly easy to handle
preferred by most
designers—a close
second choice

Cutter
more costly
complex
versatile
reasonably efficient
complex to handle
better suited for
larger ocean-
cruising vessels

Cat Ketch
more costly
reasonably simple
fairly versatile
reasonably efficient
fairly easy to handle
a good rig for 20-footers
and up

Ketch and Yawl
most costly
most complex
very versatile
less efficient
complex to handle
better suited for larger
ocean-cruising vessels

Schooner
most costly
most complex
fairly versatile
least efficient
complex to handle
more a nostalgic choice
than a practical one
for a small boat

Sail Shapes

The Square Sails

By far the oldest and most used sail shape, historically, is the square sail. For running downwind, it's still the best. Perhaps the Vikings were the world's best square-sail sailors. By using what they called a *beitass* pole to hold the windward clew out against the wind, the Vikings could actually tack. Our term "beating to windward" comes from that pole they used.

The Traditional Sprit Sail

The Greeks or the Romans were the first to modify the square sail for better windward work. They moved the mast into the bow and hung the sail behind it like a flag and

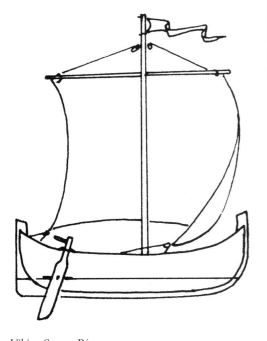

Viking Square-Rigger

Developments of the Square Sail

Traditional Sprit
very handy
fairly efficient
fairly easily reefed

Lug Rig
handy
fairly efficient
fairly easily reefed
unstayed or simple
   stays

Boom and Gaff
awkward at times
fairly efficient
can be awkward to
   reef
simple stays

supported the loose upper corner by running out a diagonal pole called a *sprit*. By pulling the sprit up against the mast, the sail could be collapsed easily and spiral-wrapped around the mast when not in use. This concept is so simple and handy that traditional watercraft use it still.

Although the sprit is less weatherly than a modern sail, it *will* sail into the wind fairly well. It has no boom to crack anyone on the head (although a flapping sheet block will) and its simple furling is easy to love. The sprit

This standing lug sail is boomless, making the rig simple. No one can get clobbered by the boom this way—but watch out for the sheet block at the unsupported corner of the sail! (Drascombe Skaffie)

can be reefed by lowering it on the mast and tying a reef around the soft foot.

The Lug Sail

An even simpler development of the square sail was the lug rig. Imagine a square sail cocked at an angle with one loose clew tied tight to the base of the mast and the other one left free to be handled with a sheet like a fore-and-aft sail. One can easily imagine this as an on-the-spot improvisation by some ancient mariner. A tomb painting in ancient Haifa, Israel, shows such a rig. Like the sprit, the lug has persisted into modern times. The sail shape is no longer square, but cut with a higher peak. The Chinese developed a fully battened lug sail in classical times that we call the *junk rig*. This variant reefs so easily that many modern sailors have adapted it for their use. The concept of full-length battens to "domesticate" a sail has been applied to modern sails, too, with great success—especially with tall catamaran rigs.

The Boom and Gaff

This was the last variant of the square sail before the triangular sail came into use. Not only is the rig aesthetically pleasing, it also offers the virtues of a short mast, a simple system of stays, and a simple emergency reefing option. By simply letting the peak of the gaff down, one can "scandalize" the sail to one-half its working area. This was an old sailors' trick when caught in a sudden squall—and it still works. The boom and gaff can, of course, be reefed properly by lowering the sail and tying a panel off around the boom. With its low profile, the boom and gaff lends great stability to the boats that use it, and for that reason it is still preferred by many.

There are disadvantages to the rig, too. The boom and gaff, even with the peak pulled up tight, cannot outpoint a modern sail, all things being equal. There is more complexity aloft and more weight and hardware where you least want it—high above the deck.

The Triangular Sails

The Lateen Sail

Ancient Egyptian art shows a variant of the square sail in use on the Nile. There is the usual yard at the masthead to hang the sail, but the sail shape is triangular with its bottom corner tied to the base of the mast. I'm guessing that this rig was adapted, as was the lug, by some enterprising seaman who untied the clew from the base of the mast and led it aft, causing the yard to swivel down in the familiar manner of the Arabian *dhows*. Such a sail would vastly improve windward work, although even the modern Arabs, who still use the rig, say that "only a fool or a Christian sails to windward."

The "modern" lateen is most commonly used on very small daysailers. Although little can be done to control its sail shape, the lateen has a very low profile that lends great stability to the boats that use it. A small sailing cruiser could be easily converted to use a single lateen sail. The lateen rig does sweep the deck area ahead of the mast, however. This could make anchoring and other forward work awkward.

The Bermuda Sail

The purely triangular, or *Bermuda*, sail is a relatively modern innovation made possible by improvements in rigging and mast construction. In earlier times, the tall Bermuda-rig

Developments of the Arabic Lateen Sail

Lateen Rig
very simple
good for "tippy" boats
fairly efficient
simple to reef
usually unstayed

Modern Triangular Sail
simple
most efficient
easy to reef
usually stayed,
    sometimes stays are complex

Wishbone Rig
fairly simple
efficient
reefing easy, but system
    can be complex
usually unstayed

mast wouldn't have held together long. There is a variety of "go fast" adaptations to control sail shape and thus improve speed. Triangular sails are easily reefed with reef points or by rolling part of the sail around the boom.

The Wishbone

Some of the earliest triangular sails used in this country didn't have booms at all but used sprits. Whereas a sail full of air will lift the boom, causing a pocket to form and spoiling sail shape, with a sprit the lower edge of the sail holds the tip of the sprit down (like a vang) and sail shape can be controlled simply by adjusting the tension of the sprit. The simple elegance of this concept is spoiled only by the disturbance in the sail shape caused by the sprit itself when, on one of the two windward tacks, the wind presses the sail flat against the sprit. The wishbone solves that problem by being curved, thus not spoiling the sail's shape. On little boats, though, the straight sprit can be laid against the mast and wrapped up with the sail. This is a clean and neat system of furling.

Reefing sprit rigs is trickier. Most small boats reef by rolling part of the sail around the mast. Some gather a slab of sail against the mast with lines called *brails*. Such a system is simple and fast.

Summary

The most common small-boat rig is the sloop with modern triangular sails. It does most things best. For a small catboat, I think I'd try a triangular wishbone rig. For ultra-simple knocking about, I'd prefer a traditional sprit or maybe a lateen—especially if my boat was tender and I wanted my center of effort as close to the water as I could get it. One nice thing about a really small boat: You can almost afford to experiment, try things out, see what works best. You might like two different rigs for different conditions so you could take your pick. Before you destroy anything on a stock boat, though, bear in mind that the hull and rig were designed to go together. I would have a good solid reason before I made a change.

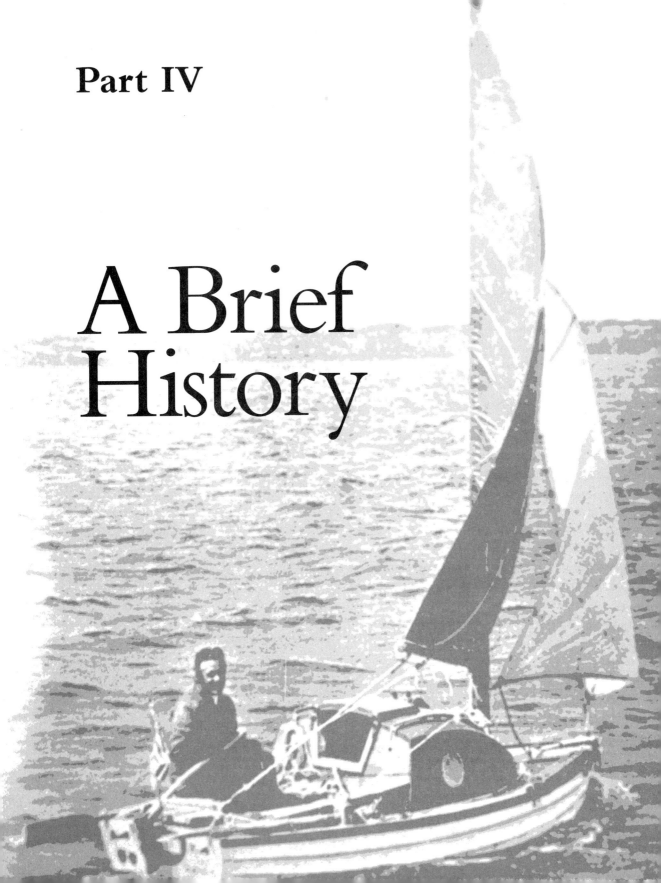

Part IV

A Brief History

How It All Got Started

The Pleasure of Being There

Boating for pleasure is hardly a new idea. Cleopatra enjoyed occasional excursions up and down the Nile on an elaborate gold-leaf galley driven by twin banks of oarsmen. In yachting terms, it was the original "gold plater." (I've seen some opulent powerboats go muttering by and waited in vain for one of them to have *Cleopatra's Barge* emblazoned on the transom.) The magnificently carved Osberg ship was believed to have been built as a pleasure boat for a Norwegian queen sometime around 900 AD. Going to sea for the sheer pleasure of it seems always to have been a natural thing to do.

There is a difference, though, between going in style and putting out to sea in a very small vessel with few, if any, amenities. Roughing it for fun seems to be a more recent development. It's worth a guess that only since creature comforts became commonplace that going without them has taken on a novel charm. For many who earn their livelihood at sea in small boats, the idea of gratuitous sailing in small boats has seemed odd and a little comical. Still, working sailors were the first to participate in sport sailing—racing.

Getting Somewhere in a Hurry

Getting somewhere in a hurry has long been a Western preoccupation. Cargo vessels paid a premium for fast voyages, and some of the

great clipper ships competed over courses that took them to markets halfway around the world. As races go, these were without a doubt the most spectacular and thrilling of all time. We will never see their like again.

On a more modest level, fishermen have always competed to be first at the market with their catch. The pressure to develop vessels both rapid and capacious laid the groundwork for modern yachting. Well over a hundred years ago, owners of fishing vessels staged formal races just for the pride and pleasure of seeing whose boat was fastest. It was just a modest jump from those contests to the first yacht races between boats built by private owners—for their pride and pleasure. There it was: The fisherman built his boat to *earn* money with it, while the yachtsman earned his money doing something else and got a boat to spend it on. So it has been ever since.

Exploring and Adventuring

When white men first began exploring the North American continent, they rapidly grew to appreciate a traditional native form of watercraft—the canoe. In a country so rich in waterways, the canoe was the ideal vehicle of exploration: light, shallow draft, and swift. The canoe rapidly took on a romantic aura and became a powerful symbol as well as a practical vessel. Here was something simple and affordable, not just for the rich but for everyone. With a canoe, one could go exploring, pack a tent, and feel a little like Lewis and Clark, Radisson, or even Hiawatha. Soon folks were adapting sailing rigs to canoes and the final ingredient for the modern yachting scene had been added.

What have we got? We have the simple pleasure of just being out on the water...we have the pleasures of racing and competition ...and we have the pleasure of adventure, of travel, of exploring new places, even if they're only new to us. In one proportion or another this explains what sailors get out of sailing. All of these pleasures are obtainable in small boats. Let's look briefly at some of the highlights of the history of small-boat pleasure sailing.

The Birth of Small-Boat Cruising

N. H. Bishop
In 1885 a writer for *Forest and Stream* magazine named N. H. Bishop conceived of the idea of sailing in a tiny sailboat from Pittsburgh all the way to the Gulf of Mexico via the Ohio and Mississippi river systems. The vessel he chose was a *sneak box*, a small, very shallow-draft boat originally developed in New Jersey for duck hunting on Barnegat Bay. Nicknamed the "floating coffin" in 1836, the sneak box was fully perfected by Bishop's time. The hull itself was rounded and flat, rather like a spoon. The deck, like the bottom, was rounded too—highly crowned. A daggerboard was mounted well off-center to leave the floor clear for a hunter to snuggle down inside the hull for the night. Imagine spending the night *under* your bed and you've got the idea. In such a cramped but nimble vessel Bishop set out for the Gulf. He made it and published the account of his adventures in a book, *Four Months in a Sneak Box*.

Seneca
Bishop's adventures prompted another *Forest and Stream* writer ("Seneca" to his readers)

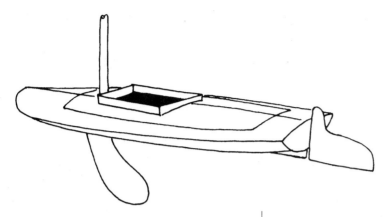

A "sailing coffin," a Barnegat Bay sneak box
(H. I. Chapelle, American Sailing Craft)

up by necessity pioneering the techniques of sailing single-handed. By the end of his career he had logged 19,000 miles at sea. He was found dead at the tiller, finally, while his boat drifted quietly. The year was 1891. McMullen kept careful accounts of his experiences and left a rich legacy for others to follow, hopefully with a lighter heart.

to undertake sneak-box voyages of his own. These stories did much to promote public interest in small-boat cruising in the United States.

Meanwhile, Robert McMullen was getting the hang of cruising in somewhat larger yachts in England. It's hard to figure out exactly what pleasures McMullen got out of sailing. Rigid, puritanical, fanatically organized, McMullen seems to have sailed as an exercise in self-discipline. He exasperated even hired crews and, consequently, ended

MacGregor

Another Englishman, Captain John Mac-Gregor, disabled from a railway accident, designed a series of light, shallow-draft double-enders, which he called "Rob Roy" canoes, and sailed them more than 1,000 miles through the waters of England, Scandinavia, Europe, and Palestine. His boats, resembling sailing kayaks, gained an instant following after the publication of MacGregor's book, *Canoe Travelling,* in 1881. Clubs sprang up in England and, in the late

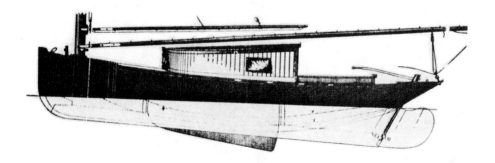

The Coot, *the South Bay catboat that C. P. Kunhardt cruised 1,600 miles from New York to Beaufort, North Carolina, and back again between November 1885 and July 1886*

1800s, the New York Canoe Club was founded. Rob Roy canoes were easily adapted to racing and soon competition, even between clubs across the Atlantic, became fierce.

The Rob Roy yawl, "the poor man's yacht," under sail

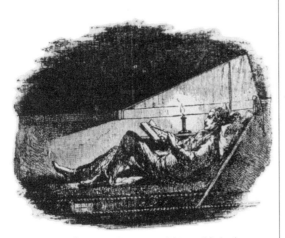

Captain John MacGregor and his published accounts of cruising on the Rob Roy started a national pastime. He added his design concepts to the new field of small-boat architecture.

Middleton

Still another Englishman, Lieutenant Middleton, circumnavigated England in a Rob Roy canoe in 1869, inspired by another MacGregor book, *A Thousand Miles in a Rob Roy Canoe.* Middleton then did a rather obvious thing. He began to wonder what it might be like to sail in something just a bit bigger and more comfortable. Remember, there simply weren't any small pleasure boats, with the exception of the Rob Roy, being built anywhere. Middleton adapted a 17-foot fishing boat to his purposes and went on sailing, experimenting, and writing. McMullen, MacGregor, and Middleton had one thing in common: None of them started off as

Alfred Strange, 1856–1917, small-boat sailor and innovator

Illustration by Strange of his Cherub II *yawl*

experienced seamen, nor could they have gotten much sea lore from reading. They were, in fact, "writing the book" themselves.

Strange

Picking up where Middleton left off, Alfred Strange, a skilled marine artist as well as sailor and designer, designed a series of compact sailing cruisers. By the time Strange died in 1917, pleasure sailing had taken root in both Europe and America. Many traditional small working craft had been adapted for sailing or for racing, even as the commercial necessity for their existence was passing. Many small builders have preserved the sharpies and dories and traditional catboats—though mostly in fiberglass now. MacGregor, Strange, and Middleton all shared the dream that sailing and cruising might be enjoyed, not only by the affluent, but by everybody. In

vessels and materials they had never imagined, those dreams have come true.

Tiny Ocean Voyagers

Early Voyagers

Every year or so we read about someone crossing the Atlantic in a tiny 6-foot boat. People have been working on that "smallest ever" record for more than a hundred years.

In 1876 Alfred Johnson sailed his 20-foot dory *Centennial* across the Atlantic in a rugged 46-day passage. *Centennial* Johnson's accomplishment ignited a fervor for small-boat passages. The next year, Thomas

Alfred Johnson

Attempting to convince a shark it's time to move on, Johnson stabs at it with a knife tied to an oar.

Crapo of New Bedford sailed his 19-foot schooner-rigged dory across the Atlantic. He subsequently drowned in 1899, en route from Newport to Cuba in a 9-foot vessel.

In 1880, two gentlemen sailed their 16-foot cutter *Great Western* to England, returning the following year. Eighteen-ninety-one saw Josiah Lawlor sail his 15-foot sprit-rigged *Sea Serpent* in a transatlantic race against William Andrews. Andrews' 15-foot gaff sloop capsized and a nearby steamer picked him up. Lawlor made it in 45 days. The following year Andrews did too—in a new boat, the 14-foot *Sapolio.*

Modern Micro-Voyagers

Clearly, small boats can be seaworthy. Nestled down between ocean waves, they often dodge large seas that mercilessly pound larger vessels. However, if caught under a breaking wave, a small boat can be instantly smashed

William Andrews and Sapolio

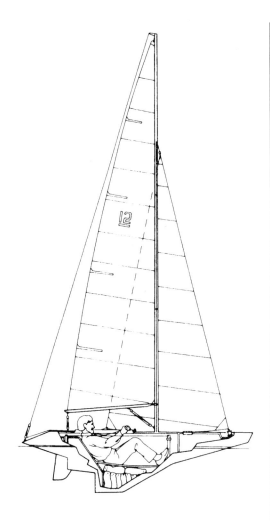

under tons of seawater. Gary Spiess examined the remains of the 11½-foot *Little One* in his book, *Alone Across the Atlantic.* William Willis perished in *Little One,* attempting the voyage Spiess was about to undertake in an even smaller boat.

> *I could see that the* Little One *had suffered a lot of damage. Her mast and boom were gone, a chainplate had been sheared off at the deck and bare wood was exposed in several places where the fiberglass had been torn away. Part of her keel*

was also broken. . . . I stared into the cabin transfixed. Questions crowded my mind. What had happened to Willis? Had he slipped overboard? Had he fallen into such a deep depression that he'd taken his own life? Why hadn't he kept a log—or if he had, why had no one found it? And would Yankee Girl *and I suffer the same fate?*

Spiess, in his 10-foot boat, survived his 1981 Pacific crossing. Others have not been so fortunate. After successfully crossing two oceans, John Riding and his 12-foot *Sjö Äg* vanished in the Tasmanian Sea.

At this writing, the smallest East-to-West voyager is Eric Peters' 5-foot, 10-inch sailing "barrel," the *Tonky Nou.* He crossed in 1983 in 46 days. The smallest West-to-East passage was completed in 1983 also, by Wayne Dickinson, who sailed his 8-foot, 11-inch *God's Tear* across the Atlantic in 142 days to prove, he said, the existence of God.

What is, in fact, proved by all this? Is this cruising? I couldn't and wouldn't want to take anything away from the courage and endurance of these men and the generous courage of their families who also sweated out their passages. But these feats seem to me to have been stunts, tests to tempt destruction of the men and their boats. For the men so tested, the experience surely must be an incredible high. I'm reminded, however, of Robert Manry, who sailed his 13-foot *Tinkerbelle* across the Atlantic in 78 days during the 1960s. Suffocating in his job as the classified-ads manager for his Cleveland newspaper, Manry modified his family boat and put out to sea. We saw him at last in Falmouth, England, embraced by his family and surrounded by a jubilant throng of well-wishers and admirers. After all this time, I still

Robert Manry nears England after 78 days at sea.
(Plain Dealer *photo by William A. Ashbolt*)

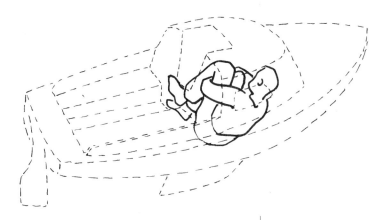

The mariner attempting an epic voyage in an undersize craft can anticipate up to 90 nights curled up like this in a cabin already crammed to overflowing with provisions.

remember him, arms outstretched, frozen in his moment of triumph. But then what? The boat was crated and shipped home. Manry returned to his desk at the *Plain Dealer*. But how do you return to ordinary living after such an experience?

Questing Versus Cruising

There's a distinction to be made here, subtle but important, between cruising and questing. The cruising sailor who voyages from place to place in a small boat is savoring an experience for its own sake. He, or she, not only enjoys the sail but, upon arrival, lingers to see the sights, meet the people, sample the cuisine. Surely the accomplishment of getting there is a real part of the satisfaction, but only a part. The next cruise could be to anywhere—anywhere at all. But if one's object is to break a record, to generate publicity, *simply to have done it,* then what can be next?

One examines the map for a larger body of water, a more dangerous location. Cape Horn. The Arctic. How will it all end?

I like Lin and Larry Pardey's approach. As they left California on their boat, someone on the dock called out, "Where are you going?" "We don't know," they replied. "How long will you be gone?" the voice called. "As long as it's fun." I like that.

If you own a small boat or are thinking of getting one, I would urge you not to get swept away by the lure of using it for some epic purpose. Most small-boat manufacturers will be the first to tell you that their 17-footer was not designed for extended ocean cruising. You can test your capacity as a sailor to the limit without exceeding the design limitations of your boat while exploring countless rivers, lakes, bays, and coastlines. There are real and deep satisfactions to be found in singlehanding, but I would hope they would not, for most sailors, undermine the boat's role as a focal point of *family* adventure and togetherness.

The Legendary West Wight Potter

In 1949 Colin and Stanley Smith built themselves a 20-foot sailboat, *Nova Espero,* in the basement of a chapel in Halifax, Nova Scotia. Being short of money, they lashed a dinghy to the foredeck in lieu of a cabin and set off for England, arriving in 44 days. Two years later, Stanley Smith sailed an improved version across the Atlantic again, in company with Charles Violet, to celebrate the 1951 Festival of Britain.

One can't spend more than four months at sea in a small boat without forming some pretty strong opinions about boat design. Stanley Smith settled in England and, on the stormswept Isle of Wight, designed a novel little boat to be built out of plywood. The result was a stout, pug-nosed little vessel only 14 feet long. Her hard-chined hull facilitated her plywood construction and made for a very stiff sailer. Wrote Smith:

The high shoulders forward give the boat those few extra inches of freeboard just where they are needed to discourage the bow wave from getting carried up by the wind when sailing close-hauled. The lower freeboard in the waist . . . it is at this point where we most frequently get in and out of the boat, where the natural form of the surface of the sea dips down when the boat is moving, and a green sea seldom finds its way on board here. The "kick up" towards the transom, the greater freeboard aft, is very reassuring when contending with awkward following seas. The result is a small craft which feels bigger, more compatible and safer than any other 14-foot boat.

Smith wanted a boat in which one could, for the sheer pleasure of it, venture out into even rough waters and "potter around," as the English put it. Smith designed a cabin

A Potter 14 sails itself with the tiller lashed.

that contained two 6-foot 4-inch bunks. In fact, the whole floor plan of the cabin was these bunks, divided along part of their length by a centerboard trunk. The cockpit contained a self-bailing footwell. To boost sales, Smith promised to deliver his boats by trailer or by sea, so when an order came in from Sweden requesting water delivery, Smith loaded his tiny boat with provisions, oilskins, and warm clothing and, in mid-October, set out across the North Sea. He navigated his way, sometimes through snow, through the Baltic and arrived safe and sound after six weeks at sea. Needless to say, this daring voyage did nothing to diminish either the Potter's or Smith's reputation. Soon the vessel was being produced in fiberglass on the American West Coast. Smith eventually shut down West Wight Plycraft Co., but by then the Potter was an established legend.

Some Potter Exploits

In 1970 David Diefenderfer spotted from a plane a city deep in the vast inland swamps and lagoons of east central Mexico. Launching his Potter at the end of an oxcart path near Tuxpan, Diefenderfer penetrated the maze of waterways, eventually spotting a church belfry rising out of the mist. He had found Mexicalititan, an ancient Aztec stronghold. The town boasted, despite its isolation, electricity and even movies. But no tourists. The Potter was the first North American craft to ever penetrate the jungle and possibly the last. Until his death at 80, Diefenderfer's passion was exploring the remote and untraveled waterways of North and Central America. He was planning a trip to Australia when he died.

Drawing only 7 inches with its center-board up, Diefenderfer's boat was ideal for inland odysseys. Still, it was on the high seas that Potters were to make their reputations.

In 1976 David Omick, at the age of 21, accompanied a survey team to Fairbanks, Alaska. Fascinated by the country, he planned a return trip—by boat. Confident that his Potter could survive the trip, Omick set sail from Seattle, bound for Ketchikan 1,000 miles away.

In Queen Charlotte Sound his little boat was battered by 50-knot winds and 20-foot waves. Twice David was washed overboard only to be swept back to his boat on the next wave. Relying on coastal piloting skills, Omick spent 90 days working his way up the coast, exploring hundreds of scenic inlets and harbors. He is believed to be the first to have made that rugged passage alone and in so small a boat. Maybe Omick had heard, by then, of John Van Ruth.

Van Ruth, of Tucson, Arizona, purchased his Potter in July 1969. Soon Van Ruth was trying his boat out in the Gulf of California, learning and gaining confidence. Sailing off the Mexican coast again in 1971, Van Ruth was caught in a storm. He writes:

The wind picked up the morning of departure, and we tacked all the way to Isla San Esteban. The next day the wind was much stronger so I decided to stay there another day hoping it would diminish; it didn't. Just before sunrise, Freya's anchor broke and we went up on the rocks; somehow I managed to get her off after a nightmare struggle and hard paddling. I hoisted the jib and got away from the island. Freya was holed on the port side, her rudder was sheared off level with the bottom of the transom, and the engine was smashed beyond repair. The outboard bracket was hanging by one arm and the motor was underwater. I kept bailing and I was moving southwest with the current and wind.

At first I tried to make a rudder out of my paddle by lashing it to the transom. Finally, I got an idea and used the companionway hatch, cutting off the small piece and a crescent section off one corner, then drilling a hole with a whittling knife for the bolt. With little effort I took out the old piece of rudder and bolted the new one on—it worked beautifully. The rest of the trip was a very cold and rough one. I had never been in stronger winds, the tops were blown off the waves, and I was soaked for 14 hours or so until we arrived at land.

Convinced that his little boat was safer than a larger yacht, Van Ruth departed from Puerto Vallarta in 1972 and arrived safe and sound in Hilo, Hawaii, 80 days later.

Freya *held up very well. I have cleaned and inspected her hull for cracks but none are present. I was chiefly worried about the ability of the hull to hold up (when close hauled) to oncoming seas and then when she fell into troughs. At one time we hauled continually for five days (short 1 hour) with tiller locked and under main only. She self-steers very well close hauled. We made our best day's run of roughly 75 miles . . . I met with no storms but it did become quite rough at times. I honestly believe that sailing a Potter from the Americas to Hawaii is much safer than driving a car the same distance on land.*

These voyages differ in one respect from many of the midget ocean crossings that have made the papers: They were actual cruises that were, only incidentally, made in such tiny boats. The navigators had simply used the boats they already owned to go exploring. We pause to look at the West Wight Potter because it represents the first of what eventually became a whole breed of sailboats. After 20 years, the Potter enjoys a continued success in the marketplace, but it is not alone. There are probably at least 40 small sailing cruisers of various kinds on the nation's waterways keeping it company. For the rest of this book, let's look at some of these and consider their applications and their merits.

Part V

The Boats

In this section, we're going to take a look at small sailboats suitable for cruising. It's impossible to have an organized discussion about small boats without some system of nomenclature by which boats can be grouped and classified. Clear distinctions are often hard to make, but we'll proceed with the following broad categories:

Micro-Cruisers	2 bunks; very light weight
Compact Cruisers	4 bunks; weight about 1,000 pounds
Family Weekenders	4 to 5 bunks; weight between 1,800 and 2,500 pounds
Open Cruisers	no fixed cabin
Small Cruising Multihulls	catamarans and small trimarans
Maxi-Trailerables	usually 4 bunks; the largest boats we'll look at in this book

We'll also look at boats you can build from kits and boats you can build from scratch or rescue from oblivion as they rot away in boatyards and junkyards. Some of these boats are no longer in production but can be bought at a good price on the used-boat market. As a potential boat buyer, you have an enormous range of choice.

A Taxonomy of Small Cruising Yachts

Micro-Cruisers

General Description

A *micro-cruiser* is a small sailboat with a cockpit, an enclosed cabin, and two permanent inside berths. These boats are usually 14 to 16 feet long and weigh between 450 and 900 pounds. In such boats, one person can sleep on one berth, stow gear everywhere else, and sail astonishing distances in absolutely no comfort at all. Seriously, the long-distance mariner is caught in a double whammy with a micro-cruiser: Accommodations are minimal and, with such short waterlines, speed is minimal, too. One must thus spend maximum time at sea in a boat offering minimum comforts. But let's face it, most people don't buy these boats to cross oceans in them. Most micro-cruisers are purchased to be used as daysailers, and many of their owners have never even spent a single night aboard. More's the pity.

A solo sailor can cruise in a micro-cruiser for a week with no trouble at all. Two people can sail without replenishing supplies for two or three days if they require no privacy and enjoy camping out on the water. That's what you do in a micro-cruiser—you camp out. If you think of the cabin as a permanent fiberglass tent, you'll have the idea.

A family of four can daysail happily and find enough privacy in the cabin to go to the bathroom or wriggle out of wet bathing suits. In most weather, a boom tent or Bimini top can convert the cockpit into a sleeping area for the kids.

In summary, with a micro-cruiser, you get really effortless trailering and launching, extended cruising for one, short cruising for two, and, with enormous forethought, weekending for a family.

The ideal way to extend the capabilities of this kind of boat is to trailer it from place to place, sailing a day or two here, a day or two there. You can use your car or van to complement your storage and sleeping accommodations, shop when you need food, and otherwise vary the routine. Tents carried aboard can often permit a night or two ashore while you're cruising. You can do more in these boats, I'm sure. People have, but I think you'd be stretching your capacities and the boat's to try to do too much more than its designers intended.

The Peep Hen 14

    Length: 14'2"

    Beam: 6'4"

    Draft: 9"/3'

    Weight: 650 lb.

    Sail area: 115 sq.ft.

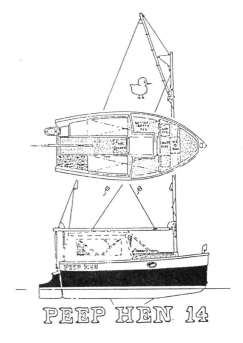

PEEP HEN 14

As legend has it, this little boat was the whimsical product of a New Year's Eve's doodle on an upturned napkin. The pen was wielded by the ingenious Ruben Trane, who wanted to know what a micro-cruiser might look like that could accommodate his ultra-tall frame—sleeping, sitting, and out in the cockpit. He'd decided in advance that he wanted to do all this in only 14 feet. Oh yes, he wanted to be able to cook in the cabin and go to the bathroom in comfort, if not in dignity. All this he accomplished in this shoal-draft, flat-bottomed catboat.

The boat is, admittedly, a little odd. Still, Trane solved all the problems nicely. A shallow box keel provides a footwell and a runway for the portable toilet to slide out from under the cockpit to a ventilated spot under the main hatch. With Ruben's height, perhaps his head stuck out to where he could rest his chin on the main hatch and survey his

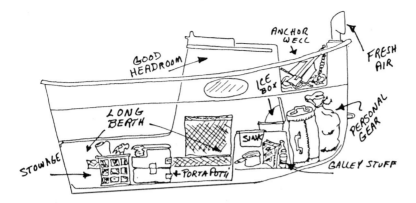

above the boom, so the whole rig stays in place for trailering and sets up swiftly. There is an anchor well forward of the cabin big enough to house a child or two. The cockpit is spacious, with an outboard well molded into the transom. A boom gallows offers sail-handling practicality as well as a framework for a cockpit enclosure (complete with screens) for those who might wish to sleep children out there, or have more room for themselves.

The builders will be the first to tell you that the flat-bottomed Peep Hen is designed primarily for protected waters, and in that setting there's more liveability per foot here than in any other micro-cruiser. Some other designs offer more seaworthiness, perhaps, but at the expense of interior comfort. This is a clever, if unorthodox, concept—well executed.

surroundings. Lesser mortals would find full headroom and then some, even on the throne. A centerboard trunk fit against one side of the box keel. Sleepers fit half in the cabin, half under the cockpit seats. A transverse galley counter occupies the forward end of the cabin, with an ice-chest insert. Forward of that is a storage bin. Useful space is impressive in a boat so small.

Topsides, the cat-rigged boat is driven by a boom-and-gaff sail. The mast hinges just

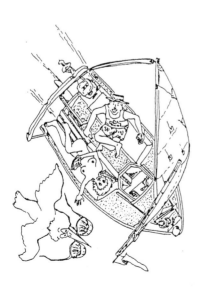

The West Wight Potter 15
> Length: 15'
> Beam: 5'6"
> Draft: 6"
> Weight: 475 lb.
> Sail area: 90 sq.ft.

The Potter is only 15 feet long, including the pulpit and rudder. For most of its history, it was 14 feet. It has the smallest cockpit of the three, but the most voluminous cabin. Once in the cabin, one sits cross-

The author's wife pilots a deeply reefed Potter 15 in the Canadian Rockies.

The author's lateen-rigged Potter sails in St. Mary's Lake in Glacier Park.

legged on the bunks. There is no footwell in there. On the contrary, there is a centerboard trunk. It is the only boat of the three with a centerboard trunk intruding into the cabin. There is no ideal place for a head in this boat. One must park the portable toilet in the aft starboard corner of the cabin by day and out in the cockpit at night.

At 475 pounds, the Potter is by far the lightest boat of the three. It is far and away the most lightly ballasted, too, deriving most of its stability from its hard-chined hull shape. Under sail, the Potter heels very little. The mast and rigging seem light—more like a small daysailer—and one must accept the boat's ultralight displacement to be satisfied with it.

With its 6-inch draft and its low weight, the Potter is extremely easy to trailer and launch. Aesthetically, it's a character boat. Some people are going to find its hard chines and exaggerated sheer odd. Others who like that sort of thing will love their Potters like no other boat they have owned—or will ever own. With the boat's reputation, it's also fun to sail into a new harbor and be asked if you sailed it from England.

The Com-Pac 16

Length: 16'

Beam: 6'

Draft: 18"

Weight: 450 lb.

Sail area: 120 sq.ft.

The Com-Pac 16 was designed by Clark Mills, the designer of the Optimist Pram, the Sun Cat, and the Windmill, to name a few. Unlike the other two micro-cruisers we've looked at, this one is a keel boat with a

The Com-Pac 16's shallow footwell makes sitting a little more comfortable. It's also used as a runway to pull the head out for use—or to stuff it back out of the way under the cockpit.

The Com-Pac 16 is a stable boat under sail.

450-pound shoal-depth keel. The boat draws 18 inches. Almost all its strengths and weaknesses derive from this feature.

The Com-Pac's cockpit is certainly adequate for a family of four. There's no centerboard or kickup rudder to worry about. The shallow keel permits the boat to heel easily at first, then the 450 pounds begin to take effect and the boat stiffens up. The boat's owners seem to find the Com-Pac a handy and able sailer.

Below, the layout of the Com-Pac can be compared to the Gloucester in some ways. It, too, has two long quarterberths with storage forward. You slide down into the berth with your legs tucked under the cockpit seats. When sleeping, knee room in both boats is limited, as is shoulder room. An insert or a pair of life cushions in the shallow footwell could easily solve the shoulder problem. The forward storage space is generous. You certainly can store your gear and have a place to lie down. Com-Pacs have been written up for some modest cruises. In most cases, the couples involved slept in the cockpits under Bimini tops.

The head storage in the Com-Pac is the best of the three. It fits under the companionway hatch, out of the way. It can easily stay there overnight. For use, it pulls out just a bit and one can sit comfortably with one's head poking out of the hatchway in the fresh air. Not bad.

Weighing 1,100 pounds and drawing roughly a foot more than the other two designs, the Com-Pac 16 is reasonably easy to drag around behind most cars, but is a bit more difficult to launch. One needs a good ramp. The Com-Pac has a proper "shippy" look to it, and it's proved a highly successful design. Several thousand of them have been sold.

These are certainly not the only micro-cruisers being sold, but they are representative enough so that others can be compared to them easily. All three were designed by highly competent designers and have stood the test of time and the rigors of the marketplace. Of the three, the Potter is probably the hardest to find used, and the Com-Pac the easiest, though I'm speaking from my location on the East Coast. The Potter is the only boat of

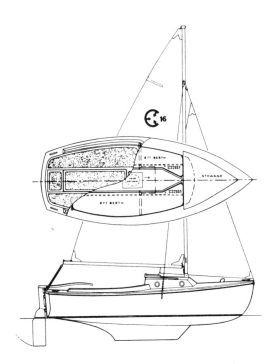

The Com-Pac 16

the three produced on the West Coast, and most owners purchase their Potters factory-direct. Being so small, this kind of boat is often a first boat—soon sold in favor of a larger boat. Short of blatant abuse (and careless beaching), these boats should be in fairly good shape when you find them used. They're not all that expensive when you buy them new.

The Gloucester 16 and the Neptune 16
   Lengths: 15'7"; 15'9"
   Beams: 6'3"; 6'2"
   Drafts: 9", 3'9"; 10', 4'
   Weights: 900 lb.; 900 lb.
   Sail areas: 137 sq.ft.; 137 sq.ft.

The Gloucester 16 was designed by the venerable Bill Lapworth. The concept has proved more durable than many of the companies that manufactured it. It's a good sailing boat, and an East Coast bargain when found used. A West Coast version is the Neptune 16. A hefty swing keel stabilizes the boats and gives them impressive windward ability. These are nimble designs with slippery underbodies. The cockpits are generous, and would-be cruisers could sleep in the cabins and adapt some open-boat solutions to food and other storage. A homemade lazarette, a big one, across the transom and into the footwell could house a complete galley, for example.

The Neptune 16, a West Coast offshoot of the Lapworth design, plies the Pacific.

The Capri 16

The Capri 16

Length: 16'6"

Beam: 6'11"

Draft: 2'5"

Weight: 1,350 lb.

Sail area: 138 sq.ft.

Built by Capri/Catalina Yachts of Woodland Hills, California, the Capri 16 is, at this writing, the largest and heaviest of the micro-cruisers. With almost 7 feet of beam and a 2½-foot-draft wing keel, she should make a capable daysailer, with lots of room in a big cockpit. At night, there are berths for two, plus storage for a large cooler and other gear in the peak. The design has a modern look without being excessively so. The 138 square feet of sail should move her smartly.

The Montgomery 15

(A good buy on the used market)

Length: 15'

Draft: 15", 2½'

Weight: 750 lb.

Montgomery boats were tough and very capable sea boats. Some impressive sea voyages have been made in a them, including a 35-day passage from California to Hawaii. The keel/centerboard arrangement provides a fairly comfortable interior with a footwell for sitting down.

The Montgomery 15

My Ideal Micro-Cruiser

    Length: 15'

    Beam: 6'

    Draft: 1½'

    Beam: 6'

    Sail area: 130 sq. ft.

It's been a long-standing interest of mine to design a small boat that would offer as much of the accommodations of larger yachts as possible. I know the great Herreshoff believed that since we don't eat, sleep, go to the bathroom, or make love standing up, headroom in a boat is a superfluity. Personally, I think there's a lot to be said for being able to pull your pants on standing up.

A trailerable boat should be serviceable on overland trips as a camper. A small boat with a standup galley would be so comfortable as to encourage its owners to use its trailerability to the full potential. Realistically, too, it is not sufficient that an idea be clever; it must also be marketable. The invitation to step down into the cabin of a 15-foot boat and stretch out on an unobstructed double-berth would be hard to resist. So headroom has been an objective. My minimums: A place to stand up . . . a galley in which one can stand and prepare something basic . . . a Porta-Potty that is not wedged in aromatically between the heads of sleeping sailors . . . and the most generous berth possible. If possible, the mast or its support should not intrude through the cabin or divide the berth.

If a boat with this interior is to be easily trailerable, it must remain shallow draft and lightweight. If it has a keel, the keel must permit the boat to be recovered from shallow ramps.

This should be a boat that encourages the owners of larger boats to ask whether they couldn't safely downsize, retaining the major comforts and reducing hassle and expense . . . and it should encourage the buyer contemplating a larger boat to forgo the horrendous expense and stay small. I'd pass up a few degrees of windward sailing for a comfortable little home on the water. It would be an honest-to-God mobile home on the road, too.

Design features. There is a strange sort of functional aesthetics going on here that I haven't the technical background to explain. Maybe I'm fooling myself, but I believe I can see what a particular idea is going to do. Modeling helps a lot in visualizing things properly, and I've been sailing, traveling, and living in very small boats for more than 20 years now. None of my credentials are on parchment, however.

A flat bottom. In specific, the design calls for a flat-bottomed hull with a bit of rocker . . . not too much forward or the bow will slap all night at anchor. With people sleeping in the V-berth, the cutting edge of the bow should be an inch or so under water; sailing with the same people aft, the bow should clear the water by at least as much. The hull offers reasonable initial stability; the ballasted keel offers complete self-righting— unusual in flat-bottomed boats. There's not more than 6 or 7 degrees of flare to the hull amidships, but there's more at the stern and especially at the bow. The bow is nearly plumb to gain waterline; the stern needs a generous rake to help lift to following seas— besides, the boat looks so much prettier that way. I've drawn the hull with a generous sheer and the transom fairly narrow. A stern that isn't too buoyant should protect the bow from digging in while running down following seas. Generous sheer in a boat is not only

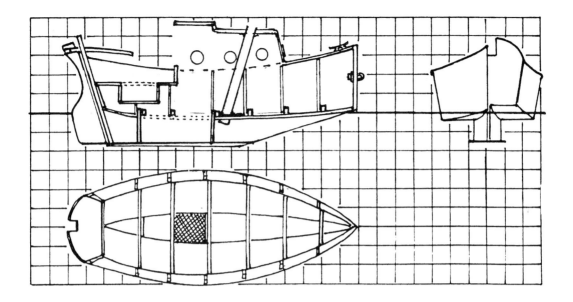

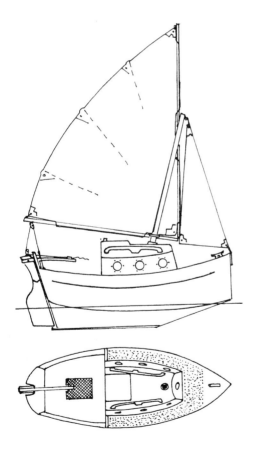

seamanlike, it's a powerful aesthetic advantage in an otherwise simple design.

A box keel. In the mid 1970s, International Marine printed a series of softcover books that were compendia of various off-beat ideas and sources for obscure hardware. They described the box keel as an innovation on Japanese fishing boats that were flat-bottomed with the motors mounted down in the box keel. Ruben Trane either remembered this idea or thought it up independently, putting it in an odd-looking little boat called the Peep Hen (see page 94). In his boat, there was an off-center centerboard. The whole package worked perfectly. I've deepened the keel to offer headroom and added ballast to offset the buoyancy of the footwell below the waterline. The boat will stand up on its bottom fairly well, too, especially if an oar is run into the sand off each side and lashed to the stern cleats. Clearly, the 1½-foot-wide keel contributes substantially to the boat's drag, but it's the ideal solution to gaining standing headroom in a small boat. The central part of the keel houses a standing well. The rest of the keel has lead, batteries, and water ballast to offset the buoyancy of the box keel.

The leading edge of the keel is gradual to facilitate its being pulled up onto its trailer and to improve tracking running downwind. The ballast almost equals the boat's empty weight, bringing the weight to 1,400 pounds. Unlike most flat-bottomed boats, this design should have good ultimate stability.

Sailing rigs. A variation of the simple lateen rig offers appealing features. If we rake the mast *forward*, we can peak the lateen up higher and gain more sail area. The mast pipe enters the cabin roof near the forward edge. The mast support pipe protrudes a bit through the bunk below. (In all unstayed rig designs, this is unavoidable. You could brace the mast with an athwartships beam at deck level. That would keep the bunk clear, but it would severely limit headroom over the bunk. Your choice.)

Simple running backstays (nylon line through fairleads to cam cleats) could provide some reassurance in heavy weather so long as they do not induce too much compression on the

mast. (Unstayed, there is no compression. I like that.)

My experience with a lateen-rigged Potter 15 has endeared me to this design in a little cruising boat. The sail is easy to raise and lower. (Being able to douse sail *instantly* is a seamanlike feature in a small boat.) In addition, reefing is rapid and simple. A singlehander can do it underway in less than three

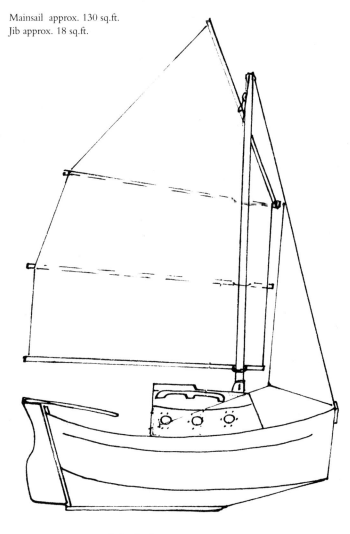

Mainsail approx. 130 sq.ft.
Jib approx. 18 sq.ft.

A junk rig

minutes. The tiller is released, the boom hauled in tight, and then the yard is let down about halfway. (The boat heaves itself to nicely while you do this.) A line from a point on the leech of the sail is drawn down and out *hard*, collapsing a pie-shaped section of the sail. The sheet is released, the yard is pulled back up as far as it will go, and that's that. It's done in as much time as it takes to tell it. The center of effort is drawn down and *aft*—which encourages the boat to point up high, even with reduced sail. A second reef reduces the sail to a wedge. The boat will heave itself to nicely with it, or you can continue underway.

We had a heavy-duty main and jib sewn by Squeteague Sailmakers of Cataumet, Massachusetts.

Five-foot battens support the generous leech without interfering with either reefing or the set of the sail when it presses against the mast on the port tack. This permits a jiffy-reefing line to run to the boom end, through a block, to a jam cleat at midboom. No adjustments to the tack of the sail need be made. With the halyard led aft to the cockpit, the first reef could be taken in under two minutes.

If the sail is pulled down completely, a tiny jib can be run up from the masthead. This facilitates running downwind in a blow that would have most folks off the water. In short, Sunfish sailors have never imagined the flexibility in their rigs—but it's there. The lateen is—surprise, surprise—an ideal cruising rig for a small boat. A Chinese junk rig could spread a lot of canvas on a short mast, or you could use a balanced lug sail. (Check out Bolger's book, *100 Small Boat Rigs*, published by International Marine; out of print but available at libraries. It's loaded with ideas.)

Sailing performance. Boats of this sort can head closer to the wind than they can drive. Windward progress, especially against a chop, is best made by easing the sheets and footing off a bit—keeping up some speed. One can check the bubbles moving by to see if there's real way on or if the boat is simply sawing up and down against the chop. Off the wind, a single-sailed boat has an advantage over a sloop: There is no loss of drive from a back-winded jib. If suddenly overpowered by a gust, the helmsman can simply let the sheet run and the sail will swing 180 degrees around and dump the wind. Only an unstayed rig with no gooseneck at the boom can get away with this. It's another safety feature. The boat should do well reaching and running. Hard into the wind will be its least favorite leg, and the helmsman will have to make sure that real progress through the water is being made. This characteristic is shared, to a greater or lesser degree, by almost all lightweight trailerable boats.

The superior interior. Below, the effect should be a bit strange, an Alice in Wonderland effect of coming down from the deck of a small boat into the cabin of a larger one. Storage bins are located under the stairs. The area under the cockpit serves for storage, with flotation in the extreme ends of the hull. There is a footwell about 12 by 24 inches long—just enough area to stand at the port-side galley to cook or shave or dress. There is a 6½-foot V-berth with no protrusions or compression posts dividing the accommodations, like Gawain's sword, into his and hers. I'd prefer to see closed-cell foam mats that absorb no water and provide additional flotation in a pinch. A Herculon cover would attach with Velcro over the mattress at night. During the day, if water got on the mats, it would be no big deal. A closet pole can run across the cabin with brackets and the mattress draped over it—making a nice backrest for lounging, eating, or reading.

Across from the galley is a storage box containing a Porta-Potty and room for a quantity of supplies. With the lid down, the box becomes a bench with room to sprawl in comfort, to read or fuss with charts. A cooler lives behind the stairs or can serve as the bottom step.

Ventilation: Beckson-brand inspection ports could serve as cabin portholes. They could be mounted from the interior with matching face plates on the cabin's outside walls. With transparent screw-in windows, the system is rugged, cheap, and waterproof.

One port faces forward; three ventilate each side. You could mount an air-scoop in the bow to better ventilate the V-berth or mount an opening hatch in the foredeck. Beckson also makes affordable plastic round opening ports with screens. After some deliberation, we used these in our boat.

Topsides. The cockpit of the 15-footer is designed for two, with comfortable lounging on closed-cell cushions, and a small self-bailing footwell. All fittings are oversized. Aluminum cleats are welded to the hull. The layout is similar to that of the small working craft that took to sea in conditions that would make today's yacht owner cringe.

Auxiliary power. It would be no big thing to mount an outboard bracket on the transom,

Brendan the Navigator *ready for the road: aluminum hull, box keel, lateen rig, electric outboard with solar recharging, mounted on a Hutchins trailer (Photo by Craig Parkhurst)*

but I would hope some sailors would prefer to row. An oar always starts on the first pull. The bridgedeck is positioned as an ideal rowing bench. We've mounted a Motor Guide electric outboard off a bracket secured to the rudder. It is silent, odorless, nonpolluting, drives the boat well, and starts at the flick of a switch. The battery, nestled down in the box keel, serves as ballast. A solar panel on the cabin roof recharges the battery. Running time per charge: 6 to 8 hours. What a way to go!

Trailering. The combination 15-foot boat and trailer should weigh under 1,600 pounds, making trailering easy—almost casual. The keel's gradual leading edge is designed to facilitate retrieval because the boat can climb back up onto the bunks. The trailer for the Com-Pac 16 fits the boat perfectly. It's plenty strong, and launching and retrieving are easy. For anyone planning to build one of these boats, this is your trailer.

Summary. This is no Flicka, but then neither would it cost $40,000. At this writing, the boat has been built in aluminum by Cape Marine of Monument Beach, Massachusetts. The interior remains to be done. We've named it Brendan the Navigator and plan global trailer-sailing expeditions. The interior space is incredible for a boat only 15 feet long. Tempered marine aluminum is practically indestructable. We have enormous confidence in what's shaping up here.

This design is, in fact, intended to do for the coastal and inland sailor what the Flicka does—at much greater expense—for global sailors. This is a simple boat and, if built that way, should be marketable for under $10,000 on a trailer. A builder with the expertise could also offer a "yacht finish" version profitably for a few thousand dollars more: col-ored hull . . . bronze fittings . . . teak embellishments above decks, wood stripping below . . . bronze ports in lieu of plastic . . . tanbark sails. She'd be pretty that way. For further information on this boat, or on variations—large and small—of this concept, write or call the author at:

Lightship Boatworks
65 Louis St.
Hyannis, MA 02601
(508) 771-5096

Please enclose a stamped, self-addressed envelope.

Compact Cruisers

Compact cruisers are sailboats with cockpits, enclosed cabins, and up to four permanent inside berths. Such boats are usually 17 to 20 feet long and weigh between 1,000 and 2,000 pounds.

In compact cruisers, one person can cruise in reasonable comfort for extended distances. Tristan Jones actually lived aboard his 19-foot Sea Dart. Shane Acton sailed his 18-foot *Super Shrimp* around the world with a companion.

Two people can, in most compact production boats, cruise up to a week—sometimes much longer. But when a family of four piles into a compact cruiser, space is at a premium. There is room to crouch in the cabin, but floorspace is minimal and everyone shouldn't expect to stand up at once. If more than two people expect to sleep in the cabin, monkey hammocks and pouches attached to the cabin walls are a must. Storage under the berths—especially the V-berth—begins to help in boats this size, but this is still minimal cruising and should be approached as such.

A family of four can daysail happily in a

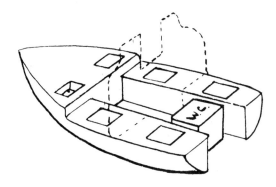

V-berth and two quarterberths.
WC (potty) under bridgedeck.
Skipper 20, Skipper's Mate . . .
Holder 20 and 17 . . . Sovereign 17 . . .
O'Day Mariner . . . Com-Pac 19 . . .
Mirage 18 . . . Slipper 17 . . .
Venture 17 . . . Starwind 19 . . .
Capri 18

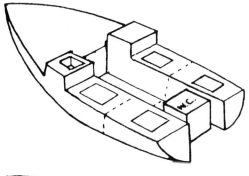

V-berth, split galley, quarterberths.
MacGregor 21 . . . Sovereign
20 . . . Gloucester 19 and 20 . . .
Freedom 21 . . . Potter 19

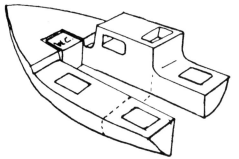

V-berth, single quarterberth, linear
galley (head locations vary).
Montgomery 17 . . . Sovereign 18

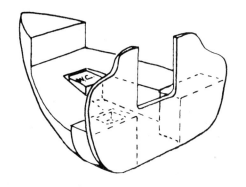

Two single berths, split galley aft.
Boston Whaler 6.2 . . . Harpoon . . .
Mystic Cat and Sloop . . . Marshall 18
Catboat . . . Cape Cod Shipbuilder's
Catboat . . . Nauset Marine Cat . . .
Drascombe's Coaster and Drifter . . .
Ranger 20

compact, but the investment (half again to twice the cost of a micro) is hardly worth it unless you really plan to put the compact's superior interior volume to use.

In summary, a compact cruiser offers voyaging potential for one, comfortable week-long cruising for two, weekending for four, and daysailing in fine weather for up to six.

Interiors

Almost all commercially made compacts offer accommodations based on the V- and double-quarterberth layout. Room is limited, so space for a head or a galley is cramped. There's really little design freedom in boats this small.

Some boats in this class offer galleys—often with tiny bowl-shaped sinks. Many such sinks are too small to hold even a dinner plate, and the first motorboat that passes sloshes the contents of the sink all over the galley. A hole cut in the countertop for a standard plastic bucket would be better. Dishes could be stored down there underway (without falling out) to be washed later. A little soapy water can even be allowed to slosh back and forth over them underway. The bucket itself is stored neatly, too. Buckets are handy on boats, but there's never a place to put them. In many compacts, cooking is best done in the cockpit. Just because everyone has an inside berth, don't overlook the cockpit. A boom tent or a Bimini can turn the cockpit into a comfortable living room, adding enormously to comfort afloat.

Most compacts have a permanent spot for the head. Beware of heads located way up in the peak. In many light boats, motion is very pronounced up there; space is cramped and ventilation may be poor.

Someone could go forward to use the head and wind up getting sick. A better location is under the companionway. One thing you've probably gathered by now, you can't be proud on a small boat. It's best to just grin and relax. Children, who often go through an annoying phase of being fascinated by their own—and everyone else's—bodily functions, will find this casual intimacy hilarious at first, and then will relax. Bathroom jokes will die down; you may grow to enjoy your kids better. Remember to thank your boat.

Some compact cruisers are designed expressly for two occupants. Most small catboats, for example, have only two bunks below. For cruising couples, this makes good sense—two really comfortable bunks and adequate storage lockers. More companies should offer a choice of interiors, one with four berths, one with only two.

Let's look at a typical compact cruiser to get an overall impression of the type, and then look at some specific features of several other boats that bear scrutiny.

The Sovereign 18

    Length: 18'
    Beam: 7'
    Draft: 1'10"
    Weight: 1,350 lb.
    Sail area: 138 sq.ft.

This boat's accommodations are, for a cruising couple, almost elegant. The head is tucked out of sight under a seat off to one side, and there is a small but serviceable galley built into the hull liner. A table can be mounted to the mast support post, another nice touch, and the V-berth is full-size and comfortable. The Sovereign, like the Skipper's

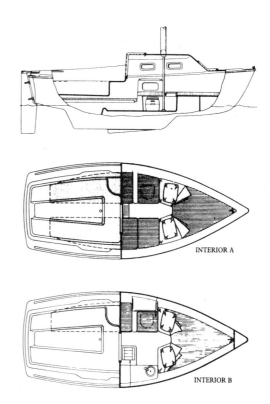

Sovereign 18 underway. Note the short bowsprit with roller to assist in raising and stowing the anchor.

Sovereign 18 interior view

Mate, has opening ports to ventilate the cabin, plus a forward hatch. Sovereign offers, for a lower price, the same hull with an interior layout similar to that of the Skipper's Mate. More companies should offer interior options like this.

The Marshall Sanderling
  Length: 18'2"
  Beam: 8'6"
  Draft: 19", 4'4"
  Weight: 2,200 lb.
  Sail area: 253 sq.ft.

Let's look at the traditional interior of a Cape Cod catboat. This one is built by Marshall Shipyard in South Dartmouth, Massachusetts. Here you have only two berths—all a couple needs—and a small galley. The head is forward. It makes sense, if you're a couple, to get an interior with only a couple of bunks. You can really move into the interior of such a boat. I met a young couple in Newport happily *living* aboard a catboat only 20 feet long. An awning shaded the cockpit. Laundry hung drying from the boom and shrouds. It was summer and they had all they needed. Another $40,000 would have bought them only more worries.

The Seaward Fox
  Length: 19'9"
  Beam: 8'
  Draft: 19"
  Weight: 1,300 lb.
  Sail area: 170 sq.ft.

The Marshall Sanderling
(Photo by Norman Fortier)

The Seaward Fox

Although the Fox doesn't look like a catboat, it offers a lot of catboat charms: enormous beam; voluminous cockpit; strong, high bow. But it's a sloop and there's no barn-door rudder to wrestle with downwind. The Fox also has some decidedly modern design features: fully battened sails and a shoal-draft wing keel. The lines suggest something traditional, even though the design was not taken off anything specific.

The Fox is faster under sail and points higher than its beamy hull would suggest. You have all that space and some speed, too. The glasswork and trim is well done, with lots of pleasing details to notice. This boat was called the Slipper 17 for many years, and various versions of the boat are available on the used market. The oldest boats, being less rounded, look all the more traditional—if that's what you like—though the finish is certainly superior on the newer ones.

The Capri 18

Length: 18'

Beam: 7'7"

Draft: 2'

Weight: 1,500 lb.

Sail area: 155 sq.ft.

There are a number of good 18-footers about: the Precision 18...the Hunter 19...and the Capri 18. All three have shoal keels with variations. The Capri has a basic keel; the Hunter has a wing keel; the Precision beats the other two on draft with a keel/centerboard combination. All three have a clean, modern look.

While all three boats have accommodations for four, compact cruisers are ideal for

The Capri 18

couples, giving them room to sleep in the V-berth and store goodies in the quarterberths. (Big plastic laundry baskets fit nicely and hold a lot.)

I've mentioned the Capri here, but if the lines appeal to you, research all three boats. I know the Capri has been sailed uneventfully to Hawaii, tracking much of the way with the helm secured whilst the voyager drank beer and read several books. So we know the Capri's a tough boat. I suspect the others could accomplish similar wonders with trusting fanatics at the helm.

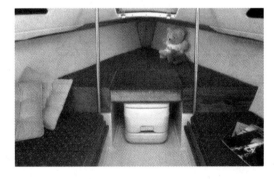

The Capri 18 interior

The West Wight Potter 19
   Length: 18'9"
   Beam: 7½'
   Draft: 6", 3½'
   Weight: 1,100 lb.
   Sail area: 181 sq.ft.

Although this boat isn't as historical as the Potter 15, it's been around a long time. The Potter 19 has more useful interior comforts than anything else in its class. That, plus the fact that it's easy to launch and retrieve, is the best reason to buy one. The high freeboard gives the 19 a dry ride with more windward ability than you might expect from such a beamy hull. The boat ghosts along quite well in light air, too.

By going to a daggerboard, the Potter people managed to provide an unobstructed standing space below the companionway hatch. Add a companionway dodger and you've got standing headroom in the cabin; you can even sail with the dodger up. If you're moving forward, you'll pick which side of the daggerboard first. The board isn't as difficult to live with as you might expect. I lived aboard one of these boats for a month while sailing the Florida and North Carolina coasts. A filler cushion makes the V-berth a comfortable proposition for two tall adults; the quarterberths are the only ones on small trailerable boats I'd voluntarily sleep in. (The Peep Hen 14's, page 94, would be a second choice.) Storage space is excellent. Monkey hammocks fit easily against the cabin's high sides for even more storage room.

With a 6-inch draft, this Potter 19 launches easily.

I'd reef a Potter 19 early. A beamy hard-chined hull gets cranky when heeled over too far. In a real blow, I'd drop the mainsail altogether and let the jib pull the boat downwind—leading it by the nose. That way, you can relax and enjoy the most boisterous weather with equanimity. On my boat, I got rid of the heavy steel daggerboard and replaced it with a plywood one. The factory had some misgivings about the move, but the broad V-bottom of the Potters is the real source of their stability anyway. With a light board, I was able to dispense with an elaborate winch-and-cable system and raise the board with a simple lanyard. Used boats can be found with a variety of winch systems, some better than others. If you're contemplating a used Potter 19, consider the pros and cons of going with a light board and, perhaps, ballasting with concrete blocks glassed to the floor under the cabinets, where they won't be seen. I've long wished the company would consider the same idea. After successfully navigating through a violent line squall in Pamlico Sound in an unballasted boat, I'm convinced of the safety of this approach.

The MacGregor 19 Powersailer

Length: 18'10"

Beam: 7'5"

Draft: 9", 4'

Weight: 1,100 lb.

Sail area: 187 sq.ft.

The MacGregor 19 Powersailer

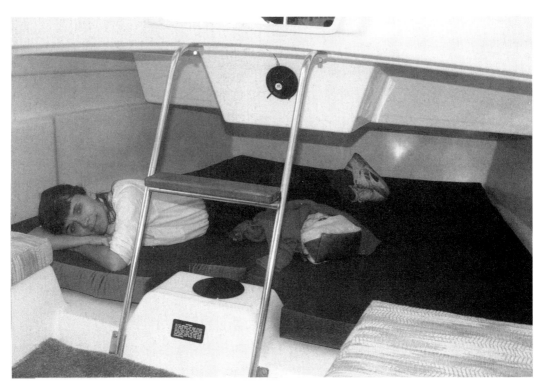

The Powersailer offers a voluminous interior. Here the author's wife, Bettina, relaxes in the generous double-berth under the cockpit.

Suppose you're new to sailing. You'd like to get out on the water, but in many ways, you'd feel more secure in a motorboat. Wouldn't it be nice to have a motorboat that did all the things you expected a motorboat to do... but then on a mild day with a moderate breeze, you could raise a mast, fly a sail, and—voilà!—you're under sail! Turn off the motor and suddenly it's quiet. The breeze gets up too much or thunderheads appear on the horizon and presto, it's a motorboat again. Such is the concept of the MacGregor 19.

Aesthetically, the 19 has nothing traditional about it. Its powerboat lines are uncompromising. Below, the boat is roomy.

The wide beam is carried all the way aft to a broad stern. There's space under the cockpit for a huge double berth. A pop-top adds to headroom under the main hatch. To starboard, there's an enclosed head—in a 19! The mast breaks into two pieces that stow neatly along the port bulkhead. The cockpit is spacious, but fairly shallow, to accommodate the bunk below. Twin rudders straddle the centrally mounted outboard. A romantic will find this boat a bit cold and alien, what with the ultramodern powerboat lines and all, but the boat works and I suspect the cabin could be romantic indeed, what with that big double berth and all. MacGregor makes affordable boats, so between price and entry-level concept, there are a lot of ideas here worth entertaining.

The Precision 18 and the Hunter 19

Lengths: 17'5"; 19'

Beams: 7'5"; 7'9"

Drafts: 1½'; 14", 4'9"

Weights: 1, 100 lb; 1,500 lb.

Sail areas: 145 sq.ft.; 165 sq.ft.

Here are two nimble boats with contemporary lines. Both boats remind me of the kind of styling one finds on modern European sailcraft. Since Hunter exports to Europe, that's no surprise.

The Precision is built in Sarasota, Florida. It's a keel/centerboard design, drawing only 1½ feet with the board up. The cabin is open and comfortable. At 1,100 pounds, this would

The Hunter 19

The Precision 21 is the big sister of the 18 and looks much like it.

be a relatively easy boat to haul around and launch—and a lively sailer underway.

The Hunter 19 is a water-ballasted centerboard design, drawing only 14 inches with the board up. It's a beamy boat at 7¾ feet. You'd get a stable and fast ride. The styling is very Euro, inside and out. A galley counter, ice chest, and battery occupy the port side; the head lives under a filler cushion in the center of the V-berth.

Both Precision and Hunter have been around a long time now. If more traditional boats look a little stodgy to you, both of these offerings are worth a look.

The Sovereign 20 and the Com-Pac 19

Lengths: 20'; 20'1"

Beams: 7'2"; 7'

Drafts: 2'; 2"

Weights: 1,700 lb.; 2,000 lb.

Sail areas: 189 sq.ft.; 196 sq.ft.

Custom Fiberglass Products of Florida has acquired the molds for a Helson-designed boat previously sold as the Montego 20 and

The Com-Pac 19 underway

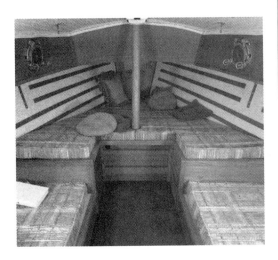

The Com-Pac 19 interior

The split galley on the Sovereign 20. Note the oversize hatchway, offering generous standing room in the cabin.

A Sovereign 20 under sail

the Express 20. They've upgraded the boat with lifelines, seamanlike teak trim, and opening ports. The quality looks very good. With a draft of 2 feet, you can get most places. The weight, at 1,700 pounds, makes her a little lighter than the Com-Pac 19, an even more traditional craft that shares the 2-foot draft. The Com-Pac 19 is still in production. Used versions of both 19-footers show up on the East and Gulf coasts especially. Both are solidly built boats; the Sovereign leans a little toward the modern, the Com-Pac toward the traditional. Your choice.

The Siren 17

Length: 17'2"

Beam: 6'8"

Draft: 8", 4'3"

Weight: 750 lb.

Sail area: 145 sq.ft.

A bargain on the used market these days, the Siren is available mostly on the East Coast and the Great Lakes. It was Canadian-built, with a swing keel to give the boat good stability when down and, when retracted, made it shoal draft and easy to launch.

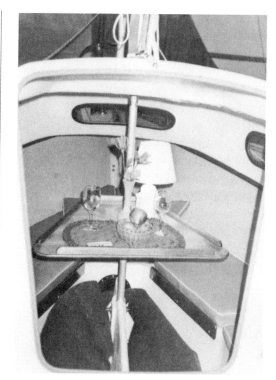

The Siren had no built-in galley unit. It did have a clever table arrangement that droped to enlarge the V-berth or raised to the overhead out of the way when not in use.

The Siren 17

The cabin offered better sitting space than sleeping space, though a couple could easily adapt the cabin to cruising, and the builder offered an impressive cockpit enclosure. The Siren sails well and, for someone on a very limited budget, could be a frugal choice. At under 800 pounds, trailering the Siren would be almost effortless.

The Skipper's Mate / Sanibel 17

Length: 17'2"

Beam: 7'2"

Draft: 1', 3'6"

Weight: 1,000 lb.

Sail area: 149 sq.ft.

Another good buy on the used-boat market. Designed by Charles Ludwig, this boat has been produced by three manufacturers. I'm mystified why it hasn't sold better. An off-center centerboard permits a footwell under the companionway hatch. There's a large V-berth forward with galley counters hidden under the after part of the bunk platform, plus two quarterberths. The portside quarterberth is extra-wide, with the centerboard trunk built into its side of the footwell. The two bunks have just adequate clearance.

Topside, it's a pleasingly traditional design, very shippy looking—and it's a good sailer besides. Drawing only 12 inches, board up, trailering is a pretty straightforward proposition.

Summary

There's an enormous variety of compact cruisers to choose from, but you do have more weight to lug around. Many can be found used, but when buying used, be sure the *trailer* has held up at least as well as the boat. Owners often totally neglect the trailers their boats sit and ride around on.

If there's a single difference that separates the compact from the micro-cruiser, it's that one camps out on a micro-cruiser and one begins to actually live (if only briefly) in the cabin of a compact cruiser. Before trading up from a compact to anything bigger, I would want to make sure I had made full use of the *cockpit* as well as the cabin first. For many sailors, a properly outfitted compact cruiser is all the boat they might ever need.

The Sanibel 17 sailing off Florida

Family Weekenders

Family weekenders range from 20 to 25 feet in length. They're designed to offer the maximum accommodations within the weight limitations imposed by trailering and ramp launching with the typical family car.

Thus, they tend to be relatively light for their size, between 1,800 and 2,500 pounds. Family weekenders are not designed as offshore cruisers, and their manufacturers would be the first to discourage you from planning, say, an Atlantic crossing in one. On the other hand, two people could cruise in more protected waters almost indefinitely or even live aboard if their boat had a pop-top for standing headroom. A family can easily go on a long weekend—or longer—in comfort.

Most family weekenders do offer pop-tops. Being able to pull your pants on standing up is nothing to sneer at. In reasonable weather, you can sail with the top up, turning your cabin into an airy and pleasant extension of the cockpit. Most of these boats also have optional galley units, a "private" space for the head, and often a table that makes into a double-bunk at night.

The family weekender is trailerable behind a full-size car; realistically, this is not a towing job for a compact automobile. A larger domestic car will handle one of these boats nicely on the interstate. In rural, mountainous country, you need a muscle vehicle. If a lot of serious overland travel will be part of your vacation pattern, a micro- or compact cruiser will be more suitable. If your overland travel is more modest, the comforts offered by this kind of boat make it very tempting.

There are a number of boats of this kind available. Let's compare in detail several family weekenders that offer distinctly different approaches.

The Catalina 22
> Length: 21'6"
> Beam: 7'8"
> Draft: 2', 5'; fixed keel 3'6"
> Weight: 2,250 lb.; keel version 2,490 lb.
> Sail area: 212 sq.ft.

The Catalina 22 interior view

The Catalina 22's pop-top provides standing headroom in the cabin.

This design by Frank Butler has proved the most successful family weekender in continuous production. More than 14,000 of them had been built as of 1983. The boat has been improved periodically since its debut in 1969.

The Catalina gets its stability through the use of a 550-pound swing keel, a heavy centerboard. It's controlled by a winch system that requires a moment's patience, but no particular brute force. The interior design incorporates the low keel housing into its design. A slightly off-center walkway provides easy access to the forward areas of the boat. The boat accommodates a family of four overnight with room for storage. A pop-top offers standing headroom.

In short, this is a well-bred, well-thought-out design, proved and perfected through years of production. It's a perennial on the used market, as well as an interesting choice new.

The Com-Pac 23

Two Comfortable 23s:
The Com-Pac 23 and
the Seaward 23

Lengths: 23'11"; 24'6"

Beams: 7'10"; 8'4"

Drafts: 2'3"; 2'1"

Weights: 3,000 lb.; 2,550 lb.

Sail areas: 250 sq.ft.; 218 sq.ft.

By the time you get up to 23 feet, there's room for some real creativity in cabin layout and decor. Here are the Com-Pac 23 by Hutchins, Inc., and the Seaward 23 by Starboard Yachts. Both are solid, traditional boats built by companies that have

The Seaward 23 underway

A look at the Euro-styled, open interior of the Hunter 23

Com-Pac 23 interior view

weathered the storms of the marine market over the years. The Com-Pac 23 has 450 pounds more ballast than does the Seaward, and 450 more pounds to trailer down the road, too. Your choice. Drafts are nearly identical; the Seaward has a wing on the aft part of the keel. The Seaward is beamier, offering more room in the boat's interior.

Both boats are finished off well in a traditional way. Both boats have forward cabins. The Seaward's is completely private, at least visually, though there are few secrets on a small boat.

The MacGregor 26
Length: 25'10"
Beam: 7'11"
Draft: 1'3", 5'4"
Weight: 1,650 lb.
Sail area: 236 sq.ft.

MacGregor had a very successful 25-foot sailboat (more than 9,000 sold). When Roger MacGregor decided to make the 26, he incorporated several major innovations into the design, principally among these is water ballast. How, you ask, can water inside the boat do the boat any good, since the boat is floating in water anyway? Granted, water is lighter than lead per volume, but when it's contained down low and the boat heels, it's lifting the weight of whatever's in the keel, be it water or wingnuts or whatever. And if the boat tries to capsize, the water is being lifted into the air—and its weight tends to roll the boat back upright. The Mac-Gregor carries 1,200 pounds of water in ballast, some 75 percent of the boat's weight in glass. So it weighs more than 2,800 pounds under sail, and 1,650 pounds trailering down

The water-ballasted MacGregor 26 underway

the road. I'd be calling this a "maxi-trailerable" were the weight actually comparable to some 18-footers.

Below, there's a huge playpen of a berth tucked under the cockpit, and additional berthing forward. Prefer to use the V-berths forward? Then you could remove the mattresses aft and stow a pair of bicycles, coolers, or even a pair of ultrashort recreational kayaks! A pop-top gives you more than 6 feet of headroom.

With a simple mast-raising system, this is a well-thought-out design at an affordable price. The thoroughness with which it renders the older 25 obsolete guarantees that this 25 will be a bargain on the used market.

The interior of the MacGregor 26 is spacious and airy.

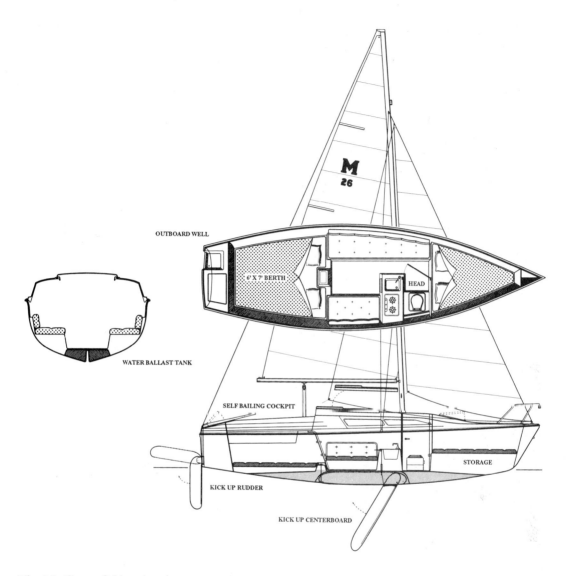

OUTBOARD WELL

6' X 7' BERTH

HEAD

WATER BALLAST TANK

SELF BAILING COCKPIT

STORAGE

KICK UP RUDDER

KICK UP CENTERBOARD

The MacGregor 26 interior view

Two Used-Boat Bargains:
The MacGregor 22 and the O'Day 22

Lengths: 22'; 21'8"

Beams: 7'4"; 7'2"

Drafts: 1', 5½"; 1'3", 4'3"

Weights: 2,000 lb.; 2,623 lb.

Sail areas: 177 sq.ft.; 198 sq.ft.

MacGregors have been sold across the country in huge numbers. I suspect at least 5,000 22s were built before the model was discontinued. Maybe 3,000 O'Day 22s were sold during the same period. This model will be most commonly found along the East Coast. Obviously, both boats were huge successes—in fact, a point arrived when it became harder to sell new boats in the face of so many used versions available at lower prices.

The MacGregor 22, with its swing keel, would be the easier of the two to ramp-launch. I owned one of these boats, used it hard, and enjoyed it immensely. With the pop-top up, there was standing headroom in the cabin. The dinette table dropped down to make a double berth; the kids slept in the V-berth forward. The O'Day 22 had a more highly crowned cabintop, offering less room than the Mac-Gregor 22 pop-top, and more than the MacGregor had with the top down. The O'Day had quarterberths in the main cabin and a V-berth behind a partition in the bow. For someone of my height, both V-berths were a bit cramped.

The MacGregor got most of its stability from its 550-pound swing keel. The O'Day had a flat bottom with rounded chines to take the visual severity off the approach. The flat bottom offered enormous form stability. Some of these boats had shoal draft (2-foot) keels, and some had keel/centerboard combinations.

Both boats had sloop rigs. I never raced one type against the other, but I suspect the MacGregor 22, running downwind with its board up, would be the faster boat. We got ours to plane a few times

and get close to 10 knots. The cockpit of the O'Day was deeper and slightly more secure; the MacGregor probably had more space. Both were good boats for a family, lots of room for a couple, and are bargains now. O'Day, even farther back, made a 20-footer (same interior layout as the 22) that would

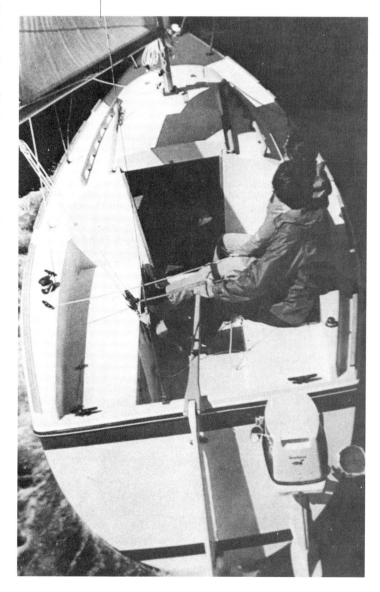

The O'Day 22 underway

be a steal if found used. MacGregor made a 21-footer of a separate design: more slender, less room below (the V-berth being the best bunk), and graceful lines. The 21 would give the J22 racer a good run for its money, I'll bet, were it tricked out for racing, too. And the 21 is a very affordable boat these days.

Summary
There is no right or wrong answer to design questions—only personal preferences. Pop-top or not; centerboard or keel; flush deck or trunk cabin; table/double or twin berths; lightweight or heavier. The choices must reflect your needs, your budget. Family weekenders offer roomy living space and comfort, and represent a serious financial investment. Naturally, the size and cost of

A MacGregor 22 underway. Note that the boat can be sailed with the pop-top up.

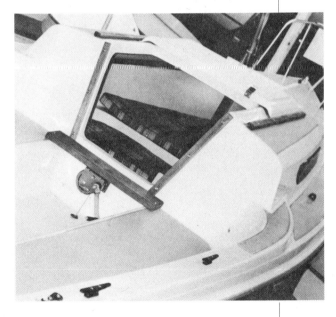

The MacGregor 21 is narrower in the beam —a fast boat. The swing-keel winch is handier mounted in the cockpit than in other models, where it's mounted inside the companionway hatch.

yachts go onward and upward, but that is not our concern here. To the contrary, I would warn only that we are at the threshold of the point where our commitments of time and money and care begin to lead us around by the nose. So long as you own it rather than it owning you, you're all right. If you can barely afford a family weekender, don't get one. Go down one size and own it outright; be carefree. If the price is not a source of worry, what the hell. Splurge!

Why Not Build Your Own?

If you're short on cash, you've probably paid special attention to ads about boat kits and boat plans. Maybe you've had ideas about getting your hands on an old lifeboat or a dory and fixing it up or turning it into an inexpensive yacht. What about that?

There's an old saying that runs something like this: "Before you start building the boat that will take you around the world, see if you can build the dinghy for it first." If you hate building the dinghy or, worse still, if you can't build it, then you've learned an invaluable lesson and paid for it cheaply. Building your own boat has a variety of meanings. Let's consider each in turn.

Fiberglass Boat Kits
A few years ago, Luger Boats in the Midwest and several other companies offered molded fiberglass boat kits of all sorts, from dinghies to liveaboard motorsailers. They are no longer in evidence, though I have hoped that someone would pick up the torch. Finished Luger boats still show up on the used market from time to time. The quality of the offering depends on the skill and patience of the builder. The kits themselves were fine. In

the hopes that during the lifetime of this book fiberglass boat kits will again be available, I'll offer a few thoughts.

If you're a good craftsman, the interior can be built to yacht standards. You can add as much reinforcement to the hull as you want—even overbuild it if you want. You have the advantage of knowing almost everything there is to know about your boat once you're done. On the other hand, if you are not a good and thorough craftsman, the interior of your boat might end up looking crude and amateurish. Should you wish to sell the boat later, you'll take a beating. If you've taken too many shortcuts, or if you're simply not handy at all, your boat might actually be unsafe. In the event of a serious failure, someone could be injured or worse, or you might be left with a boat that's impossible to sell at any price. It's all on your shoulders when you build it yourself.

I suggest there's only one really good reason for building a boat yourself: not because you'll save money; not so you can brag to your bedazzled guests that you built her yourself. No. The only good reason is you really want to do your own work. Greed or pride won't do. If you really are turned on by the idea of building a boat from scratch or from a kit, then you'll probably do a fair job of it and be content with the result. The kits themselves are all right; I don't want to imply otherwise. The issue isn't the kit, but the builder. If you aren't an experienced builder, consider not only what you might save, but what you might lose if you bungle the job.

Building a Boat from Plans
Everything I've said about kit boats applies doubly here. Only do it if you're sure you'll love the process even more than the product.

Taking the process another step, you can buy precut plywood boats for owner completion. (Friendship 14)

Here's a shippy boat built by an owner from plans: a Charles Wittholtz catboat. The designer has a whole family of boats to choose from. Note the massive air scoop forward.

There are many innovative and appealing ideas out there for those who want to work. Consider getting someone else to fabricate a small boat for you and compare the cost to a production boat. If you've fallen in love with a design, it may make sense to do it that way if you're not a good craftsman. You can personally monitor progress, suggest new ideas, and get involved sawing, sanding, and painting if you'd like. The end result will feel very personal and very special.

Buying a Semifinished Production Boat

See if the manufacturer of a boat you like will sell you a boat only partially finished. The degree of incompletion is up to you. You might catch them during a slow time in December and they might flex with you. You could maybe save a thousand dollars on a small boat that way.

Fixing Up an Old Lifeboat

Let me tell you a story. In 1974 I got this idea of buying a surplus lifeboat hull and making it into a replica of a Viking trading ship—a *knarr*. I got on the surplus bidding list and eventually some boats turned up for sale ranging in size from 18 to 36 feet.

Man and his "knarr" (Photo by Robert Anton)

View from the deck of the Odyssey. *The 400-square-foot sail and its yard were supported by two 9-foot posts. Canvas boom tents were to have stretched across the open deck both before and abaft the mast, but I was out of funds by then.*

Money was scarce, so I bid on the hulls I thought would be least in demand: the big ones. To my amazement, a bid of $125 landed me a 10,000-pound steel hull. If ever there was a pauper's route to sailing ecstasy,

this was it. A hauling outfit from Rye, New York, hauled it home to Rhode Island for $600, and there it was—a mammoth, gray, beached whale of a boat, and it was mine, all mine. It was my first boat, and I was mighty proud of it. I called it the *Odyssey*. The yacht club of Bristol, Rhode Island, watched with a mounting mixture of amusement and glee as I set to work.

The *Odyssey* was 36 feet long and 13 feet across. When I stood in its bottom, I couldn't see out. It was a very big boat, and I soon learned that time and labor and money could disappear into such a boat without a trace. Tearing out the rotted seats and the elaborate manually powered propulsion mechanism took the better part of a year of Saturdays. The inside was badly rusted. Repairing it took another year and God knows how many dozen bottles of Naval jelly. On any given workday, I could expose an area of bright metal the size of a road map.

It's an impossible task in Bristol, Rhode Island, to rustle up a crew of 20 to attend the oars, so I had to come up with an engine. I had a flywheel, a transmission, and a propeller already on the boat. To power it, I devised a transverse system of three Briggs and Stratton 5-horsepower motors, each connected by chain to the gearbox through a centrifugal clutch. Crude, but bulletproof. When the yacht club next door learned of my intentions, I could hear the laughter all the way over the back fence.

The *Odyssey*, painted dark brown outside and a burnt orange inside, was launched in July 1976. The power company had donated an enormous aluminum telephone pole for a mast. The square sail was tanbark. My father had donated God knows how much paint. The whole enterprise, including three years' storage, had cost more than $3,000— more than I could afford, less than I should have spent.

The first night afloat, a storm came up, pulled up the *Odyssey's* mooring, and sent her drifting like a vengeful juggernaut through the fleet of yachts in Bristol Harbor. The yacht club, in self-defense, tied the *Odyssey* firmly to its dock for the night. Half the club turned out the next day to see the boat motor

The Odyssey *at her Bristol Harbor mooring*

away. Each Briggs started on the first pull. The big prop churned up a boiling mass of water and the *Odyssey* thrashed its way into Narragansett Bay. As time went by, the chain drive started vibrating badly. Of three chains, one would take the full load; the rest would run slack and raise hob with the sprockets. One chain broke. I repaired it while we ran on the other two engines. Then another chain broke. We raised sail.

For half an hour we experienced the romantic joys of square-rigged sailing. Then we had to get home. We fired up the gang of Briggs and Strattons; the vibration increased. Finally all the chains let go. We drifted by a Rhode Island state mooring and picked it up. The *Odyssey* never left that mooring as long as I owned it. The drive system needed not chains, but rubber V-belts and, therefore, a whole new set of clutches and sheaves and fittings. The kitty was dry and my wife was up in arms about all the money I'd spent. Underfinanced all the way, I'd been in over my head from the beginning. Facing that was hard.

The *Odyssey* wintered in the harbor on its mooring, locked in ice. Being an open boat, rain collected in its bilges and turned to ice. Slowly the hull settled farther and farther under the load. In January, I disconnected the motors and brought them home so they wouldn't drown. When spring came, I put the boat up for sale. During the summer, I rowed a progression of folk out to the *Odyssey*. Each took in the huge investment of work and money remaining to be done and asked quietly to be taken back to shore. In the end, the *Odyssey* was given away—to the Sea Cadets. It took six months to find an organization that would even take it as a gift. It was somewhere in the midst of this expe-

rience that I developed my enthusiasm for small boats.

A Happy Story

Several years after the *Odyssey* fiasco, I had another chance at a lifeboat—this time a 12-footer. I found it in a junkyard outside Boston and purchased it for $100. It once belonged to the tugboat *Jupiter*. The hull just fit into my cellar. Over the winter, I sanded the hull down to bare metal and put on fresh paint, replaced the gunwale, refurbished the wooden seats, and made a new rudder. Still interested in square-rigged sailing, I carved a dragon's head and tail for the little boat and obtained, through the generosity of a sailmaking class, a red-and-white striped Viking-style sail. Leeboards were concealed by brightly colored shields that hung from each gunwale. To complement the boat's oar-power, I added a side bracket for a small outboard motor. Authenticity had its limits.

The finished product was christened the *Prince Val*, and was launched with due ceremony in the spring of 1978. Once it got up headway, it rowed well, and it sailed! Without recutting the sail, I tried it square-rigged, lug-rigged, and finally, moving the mast forward, sprit-rigged. The *Prince Val* couldn't point too high, but it was fantastic on a reach and downwind. Suddenly Buzzards Bay was my oyster. The *Prince Val* was simple and rugged. The dragon's head drew smiles wherever we went, and larger yachts often swung by to toss me a beer and have a gam. Best of all, the *Val* only cost me $200 or so, and thus I could experiment and learn without worrying about her much.

I made no real effort to make an overnighter out of the *Prince Val*, though I slept on her deck a night or two under a spare canvas sail. On my longest cruise, I sailed her on a 100-mile ocean trip to Newport, Rhode Island, and back. The return sail, with the main boomed out to port and the spare sail set out wing and wing, was one of the highlights of my life. The sky was a crystal blue; the southwest wind whistled up whitecaps, and we surfed down an endless progression of following seas all the way home.

Eventually I bought a used West Wight Potter and passed the *Prince Val* on (for $100) to a young chap who was eager to take his first inexpensive step into sailing.

There are derelict small boats in yards all over the country, awaiting your imagination and your love. Don't lose your perspective if you decide to rescue one of these. Keep it cheap and simple. Plan to daysail at first, then, gradually, see if you can figure out a way to

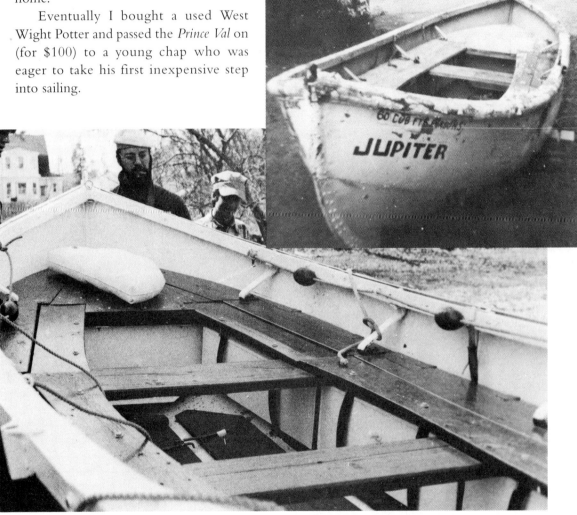

Top: Fresh from the junkyard—the Prince Val. *Bottom: The* Prince Val *emerges from its winter metamorphosis. Note the steering swivel on the stern quarter for the steering oar.*

Prince Val *under sail*

camp aboard. Keep your investment of time and money low unless the actual restoration project will be a major satisfaction in itself. Keep it fun.

If you build a boat yourself—or refurbish one—don't expect to make a killing when you resell it. Unless you're a master cabinetmaker, you'll probably get a very modest return. Price the boat to move; get your money and move on.

Check out insurance *before* you buy a kit or get started building your own boat. Make sure you can get insurance. Will the company demand that a marine surveyor examine the boat first? (At *your* expense?) With the *Odyssey*, after searching several weeks, I found a carrier that insured super tankers who agreed to insure the boat as a joke. I never bothered with the *Prince Val.* Check before you buy.

If you plan to trailer your boat, check the hull design. The Luger boats can be pur-

Two double-ended dory-like boats tied up near Lake St. Jean in northern Quebec. Sometimes boats like this just catch your eye as you drive along . . . and sometimes you can buy one for less than you had dared hope.

The fatal temptation: "I'll give it to you for fifty bucks."

chased with factory-designed trailers. A junkyard salvage job may be harder to match. The *Prince Val*, 12 feet long, weighed *800 pounds!* It would have crushed any trailer built for its size and wallowed around in any trailer built for its weight. A flat-bottomed boat might not fit a standard trailer at all.

Finally, though, take heart. If you've only got a few hundred bucks, you can get yourself out on the water. It'll take imagination and a sense of humor, but you can do it. If you can avoid giving yourself delusions of grandeur, you can even have fun.

Open Cruising Boats

J Boats, Inc., maker of the famous J-24 racers and the new J-22, did a market survey and learned that its average owner sails 55 days a year and, of those 55 days, spends only 5 nights aboard. Not much, even for a racer. It makes you wonder why the builder bothered to put in a cabin and bunks instead of, say, just a tiny private space to go to the bathroom. I suspect the company simply made a marketing decision. The public has a preconceived idea of what a boat is supposed to look like. The public expects a cabin.

What if we abandon the idea of a cabin for a while and think cleverly about this. When you're actually underway, most small-boat cabins are an instant passport to nausea and claustrophobia. While you're sailing, in nice weather at least, the cockpit's the thing—the bigger the better. Enter the open boat. The open boat can be *all* cockpit if you want, with room for everybody to sprawl or lounge around and, on a deep boat, even walk around and lean your elbows on the gunwale. If that sounds like fun, it is.

Now night falls. Bugs come out. It looks like rain—now what? Maybe you park the boat for the night and go ashore, either to your home, to a motel, or to a tent pitched on shore. That works some places, but not everywhere. Many shorelines are privately owned. You can't just sail into Marion Harbor and start toasting weenies on the Saltonstall's front lawn. Hospitality has its limits. Why not pitch your tent over the boat itself? Now that big walkaround space becomes a cabin in which to cook, play cards, and sleep. You've got the best of both worlds.

In the past several years, a number of manufacturers, mostly in Florida and along the Gulf Coast, have begun marketing some appealing open cruisers. Some have partial cabins open to the cockpit; some have decked-over sections with hatches that, when opened, reveal galleys and toilets and other practical cruising necessities. Some have dodgers that pull up like the cover on a baby carriage at night and then fold down out of the way by day. It's a wide-open field with many attractive and ingenious designs for those willing to accept alternatives to the preconception of what a cruising boat is "supposed" to look like. Let's look at a couple of designs that have gained a following and promise to be around awhile.

The Dovekie

    Length: 21'

    Beam: 6'8"

    Draft: 4", 2'6"

    Weight: 600 lb.

    Sail area: 143 sq.ft.

The Dovekie is a 21-foot vessel, the product of Phil Bolger's inventive mind and Peter Duff's molding talent and marketing courage. The Dovekie is highly unconventional and yet, in its own way, very traditional. The sail rig, a triangular sprit, goes back more than 100 years. The Dutch used leeboards 400 years ago. They're simple, efficient, and they open up the cabin interior where a centerboard trunk would be a major nuisance. The Dovekie draws only 4 inches with leeboards raised, and so will go anywhere. With such shallow draft, it's easy to row, and so oarports have been provided—an idea about 4,000 years old. The cockpit melts into a partially enclosed "cabin" that has several generous molded-in skylights. Canvas panels close up

Here's a clever idea. The Dovekie used to mount its outboard motor on the rudder. When the rudder turns, so does the motor.

The enormous interior of the Dovekie 21

The Dovekie under sail

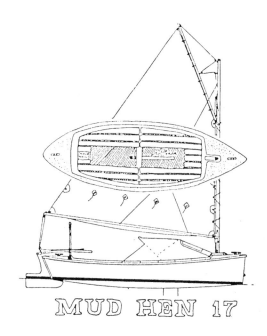

MUD HEN 17

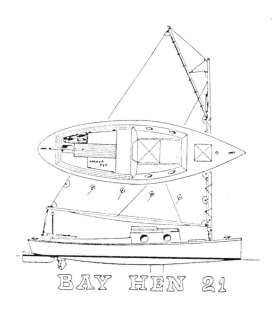

BAY HEN 21

the cabin and cockpit at night into a spacious sheltered area. The whole boat weighs only 600 pounds. There's no arguing the Dovekie is unconventional, but if you are too and the features appeal, you may have met your match.

The Hen Series: The Mud Hen 17 and the Bay Hen 21

Lengths: 17'; 21'

Beams: 6'; 6'3"

Drafts: 6", 3'2"; 9", 3'6"

Weights: 650 lb.; 900 lb.

Sail areas: 150 sq.ft.; 175 sq.ft.

The Hen series was the brainchild of designer Ruben Trane. His intent was a series of flat-bottomed, shoal-draft, centerboard boats for fairly protected waters. Three of his designs are now being produced by Custom Fiberglass

Flat-bottomed boats are easily beached.

Products of Florida. Of these, the Mud Hen is a fully open boat. Attractive teak floorboards are standard. The Mud Hen is a double-ender with an easily set up boom-and-gaff sail. The mast is mounted in a sturdy tabernacle. The length is 17 feet, the draft only inches.

The 21-foot Bay Hen has an enclosed cabin with a fair amount of space on a cushioned floor. It's a simple approach: You set it up in there the way you like. There's a huge cockpit aft. Like the Mud Hen, this boat is driven (and rapidly, too) by a boom-and-gaff sail. Both boats have a boom gallows aft to support the boom when the sail is down, and to provide a framework for elaborate tent systems that turn the cockpits into spacious living/dining areas. These are well-built expressions of some traditional approaches to small boating.

The Sea Pearl 21

Length: 21'

Beam: 5'6"

Draft: 6", 2'6"

Weight: 1,435 lb.

Sail area: 136 sq.ft.

The Sea Pearl is a traditional whaleboat or peapod shape rendered into fiberglass. Here's a long sleek hull, easy to row, easy to drive

The overnight dodger on the Sea Pearl. Note the leeboards. Sea Pearls are light enough to be dragged ashore.

under sail. The hull is less beamy than some of the other boats we've considered so far. It has an optional dodger to create overnight shelter. Like the Dovekie, the Sea Pearl uses leeboards to reduce leeway under sail.

Sailing Dories

A number of small boat shops around the country produce fiberglass and wooden dories of one sort or another. Not only are these pretty, traditional boats, the dory is a very safe and seaworthy small design.

North End Marine used to make dories up to 27 feet, some with cuddy cabins (Industrial Park, Rockland, Maine 04841; 207-594-8821). Lowell's Boat Shop has made some fine dories, too, also a "Melonseed"—a swift boat not unlike the kind Bishop and Seneca used for their inland voyages (459 Main Street, Amesbury, Massachusetts 01913; 508-388-0162). This type of boat has real growth potential, and they can be good bargains or home-builder possibilities.

The Beachcomber Dory under sail

Summary

These are some, though certainly not all, of the small open cruising boats being manufactured at the time of this writing. Many of the manufacturers are small outfits. I hope they'll grow and prosper. New companies will surely continue to come into being and those least competitive will continue to vanish. Still, the open cruising boat is a compelling concept with a lot of potential for growth. If you're looking for a boat, don't overlook this category; and if you're looking to convert an existing open boat for cruising, they offer you a wealth of ideas to borrow from.

Does this approach—the open cruiser—have any drawbacks? Certainly. Are they serious? It depends on the kind of sailing you plan to do. Many of these designs are flat bottomed—ideal for exploring coves and backwaters and hidden beaches. In rough open water, flat bottoms will pound and have a hard time of it generally. Open boats, if swamped, are not self-bailing and often are not self-righting. They may not sink, but they'll be harder to bail out. Open-water sailors may prefer a smaller self-bailing cockpit, even though they pay for it in space and comfort. Still, Drascombe, an English firm, makes a family of seagoing open boats that boast an impressive history of ocean voyages. Some of these are keel designs, others feature shallow keels and bilge keels. These boats are tough and very capable.

Some canvas dodgers protect a cabin when the boat is riding at anchor—facing the wind—but admit water when it's tied at dockside or on a trailer, when the wind and rain may come from astern.

No one approach is intrinsically superior; it all depends on what kind of sailing you

Webb Chiles almost completed an around-the-world cruise on his Drascombe Lugger, a testimony to the rugged quality of both the boat and the man. Chiles has written several books and numerous articles about his adventures.

The deep open interior of the Old World 18 offers the ultimate in daysailing. A boom tent turns this into an easy overnighter. Look at the floor space!

The Old World 18 has traditional lines and a boom-and-gaff rig.

want to do and where you want to do it. If most of your sailing will be daysailing, or if you plan to camp out ashore a lot, the open cruiser could very well be your best choice.

Small Cruising Multihulls

Catamarans

In the micro-budget category, there hasn't been much around for multihull cruising enthusiasts. The Hobie people have leaped into the breach with their Sportcruiser. A storage module stretches across the forward edge of the trampoline. Now you can store camping supplies out of the spray. A tent stretches across the whole tramp area for sitting headroom. The forward trampoline serves as a front porch. We're talking about a backpacker's lean economy here, but if travel-

The Reynolds 21

With the Hobie Sportcruiser, you can camp on the tramp.

Stiletto's optional bridgedeck tent encloses the entire bridgedeck and provides additional living space for a boatload of guests.

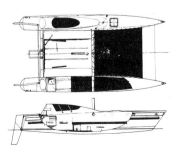

A Stiletto barrels along.

ing light is OK with you, you can travel very, very fast.

To my knowledge, the Reynolds 21 cruising catamaran is no longer in production, but it offered spartan accommodations inside its twin hulls, and blistering speed—up to 20 knots! It would be a boat to look for used.

MacGregor built a 25-foot cruising catamaran that was lightweight enough for trailering, another potential rocketship on the used market.

The Stiletto series was another well-engineered cruising cat concept—with a huge tent that connected the hulls at night. The problem for the multihull manufacturers has been cost. A lot of engineering goes into high-performance products like these, but so far the sales volume has been limited. Some good products weren't able to hang on through the later 1980s.

Trimarans

Everything that one could say about catamaran costs holds equally true—and more so— for trimarans. These designs provide a reasonably spacious central hull for more

The Argonauta trimaran outrigger

comfortable cruising. Having a central location is a little more conventional, too. Trimarans can be faster than most monohulls because with the outriggers, more sail area can be carried without fear of capsizing. The elaborate engineering that goes into the design and construction of these boats tends to make them quite expensive, considerably more, usually, than the cost of a monohull of comparable internal volume.

Tremolino Boat Company has been making trimarans for years. Their earlier products enabled the owner of a Hobie cat to use its sailing rig and hulls, mounting a central hull of their own design. At this writing, their latest model, the T-Gull, features folding amas on a 23-foot main hull, making the rig trailerable. Tremolino makes kits, too. If this approach interests you, they'll get you on the water one way or another.

Corsair Marine has a pricier series of rapid-transit

The Tremolino T-Gull underway

*The Tramp trimaran (inset). An enormous cockpit tent turned the Tramp
into a spacious overnighter.*

machines, the F-24 and the F-27. The F-24 is designed for rapid setup at the ramp, and it weighs only 1,800 pounds.

About a decade ago, an impressive small trimaran called the Tramp was marketed in the United States. It would be worth a look if one popped up on the used market.

The Tramp is an 18-foot multihull daysailer with a fair turn of speed and, with almost 15 feet of beam, unbelievable stability. It can daysail up to six and, with an optional boom tent, sleep up to four. For transportation, its outer hulls hinge downward to a folded total beam of 8 feet—a trailerable width. The enormous trampolines offer 100 square feet of lounging space.

From here on in, cruising multihulls go drastically upward in price. Like the open cruising boats, these boats, despite their high-speed allure, represent a tiny fraction of the boat market as a whole. Their general design concepts may prove more durable than their manufacturers, though I hope not. Real innovators deserve to get rich. I guess we'll see.

Why, you might ask, do multihull cruisers constitute such a small segment of the market? There may be several reasons.

Small catamarans are ideal daysailers. Most Americans will not forgo their comforts and so, though they'll spend a fair penny for a high-speed daysailer, they'll spend a lot more money for a boat they can cruise in with style and comfort. People think of catamarans as sea-going fighter planes, not as something to spend the night in.

Sailing in catamarans can be a wet and hairy experience. Little children might be scared rigid and hate it. Lacking a deep, protective cockpit, most catamarans are not considered family boats. They require athletic skill and a willingness to fly high—to take chances. That's not for everybody. Still, there's room for growth, especially if a class of cruising people develops who are willing to rough it a little to get out on the water.

Maxi-Trailerables

Over the years, some boats have been developed that are somewhat larger than family weekenders, yet are trailerable by design. I know that with the right rig, one can trailer all sorts of boats. The Nor'sea 27, a magnificent seagoing double-ender, is advertised as trailerable. By this, one might understand

For all its creature comforts, the maxi is designed for trailering. Here, the Seaward 25.

that Nor'sea Marine has made a point of solving the logistics of putting their 8,100-pound boat on a trailer and can market that expertise (and the proper trailer) along with their boat. If your sailing ambitions include meeting the ultimate wave in the Tasmanian Sea, you'll want a heavier boat than we're discussing in this book. Here we're talking about boats like the MacGregor 26 that looks like a whole lot on its trailer but, in fact, is engineered for light weight and owner setup without professional assistance. The MacGregor 26 has already been discussed in the "Family Weekender" section; what else is there?

The Kodiak 25

The Kodiak 25 (Formerly the Arctic 25)

> Length: 26'
>
> Beam: 8'3"
>
> Drafts: 16", 4'2"; keel 2'6"
>
> Weight: 3,200 lb.

Nimble Boats makes the Kodiak 25 with a pilothouse, offering you an enclosed steering station and standing headroom in a shoal-draft boat. The Nimble boats are traditionally finished off with hunter-

The Kodiak 25 interior

green hulls and tanbark sails. Below there's teak cabinetry and dark green Formica table-tops—shippy, businesslike, and well done. The trailering weight of around 3,500 pounds makes the Kodiak 25 a bit more to haul than family weekenders, but still manageable for full-size cars. For anyone sailing in rainy or foggy climes (or with a need to avoid excess sun), this is a design worth a serious look. The creature comforts are further incentive.

The Shearwater 28
  Length: 28'3"
  Beam: 6½'
  Draft: 6"
  Weight: 2,400 lb.
  Sail area: 233 sq.ft.

Edey & Duff boatbuilders of Mattapoisett, Massachusetts, introduced a big sister to their Dovekie a number of years ago. With a trailering weight of 2,400 pounds, you get an astonishing amount of living and lounging space. The beam on the Shearwater is a modest 6½ feet, making the boat a long-legged sailer and giving the interior a railway-car aesthetic. A companionway dodger could offer standing headroom to complement all the space.

The rig is split between two triangular spritsails. The big main does most of the work; the mizzen (plus the leeboards and tiny bow centerboard)

offers all kinds of subtle trim controls. With all boards up, the boat draws 6 inches! It's an easy boat to launch, considering its size. In a hard blow, one could balance the mizzen with a storm jib and be remarkably secure. At anchor, the mizzen is left standing to keep the boat from jogging back and forth all night. Everything

The sprit-yawl Shearwater 28

about the boat is well thought out and built to last.

The Sea Pearl 28
>   Length: 27'8"
>   Beam: 8'
>   Drafts: 1½'
>   Weight: 3,700 lb.
>   Sail area: 290 sq.ft.

Here's a beamier (and thus heavier at 3,700 pounds) solution to the same set of considerations that bred the Shearwater. Below, there's lots of space, thanks to the 8-foot beam. Again, I'd put in a companionway dodger

The Sea Pearl 28 interior

since with volume like this, we have almost liveaboard conditions. Water ballast steadies this design; it's one of the major breakthroughs making maxi-trailerables possible.

The Sea Pearl 28 has two masts also—a clever rig, too. Both masts hinge in massive tabernacles. The foremast hinges aft; the after mast hinges forward, keeping everything inboard. For a big boat, setting up is remarkably simple and fast. The Sea Pearl's sails are both fully battened. A keel/centerboard offers 1½-foot draft with an ultra-shoal draft version available, too.

The Seaward 25
>   Length: 25'9"
>   Beam: 8'3"
>   Draft: 25"
>   Weight: 3,200 lb.
>   Sail area: 265 sq.ft.

Built by Starboard Yachts in Stuart, Florida, the 25 is a sleek shoal cruiser with a wing keel. It weighs in at 3,200 pounds, putting it in the same weight class as the Nimble and the Sea Pearl. This is a sloop-rigged boat with traditional good looks. Designer Nick

The cat-ketch Sea Pearl 28

The sumptuous interior of the Seaward 25

Hake builds boats that are surprisingly fast for all their accommodations. Someday, I'd love to see a maxi regatta to see who's fastest. Having said that, the owners themselves would probably say that their fondness for their boats lies elsewhere.

The interior of the Seaward is bright and attractive, molding in a generous galley on the port side. A forward cabin offers privacy for sleeping, plus an enclosed head. Eight stainless opening ports, plus hatches, should make this an airy boat below.

This is an attractive, well-thought-out design. It's been around long enough for used boats to be a possibility, though the new ones are prettiest and have the most refinements—one of the advantages of a tested design.

The Flicka 20
   Length: 24'
   Beam: 8'
   Drafts; 3'3"
   Weight: 4,500 lb.
   Sail areas: 250 sq.ft.
Built by Pacific Seacraft of Fullerton, California, this is the ultimate small boat,

Very high priced but, at 20 feet, maybe the ultimate small boat: Pacific Seacraft's Flicka

Liveaboard potential in 20 feet: the Flicka

capable of crossing oceans. It's designed to carry a good load of supplies. (You could have pulverized my old MacGregor 22 and poured the remains into the Flicka's bilges just to bring her down to her designed waterline.) On the other hand, a new Flicka costs more than all the boats I've ever owned put together. I mention the design here out of sheer admiration of its robust construction, standing headroom, and shippy appearance. It's always been in the back of my mind as a sort of archetype—like one of Plato's ideal forms. You can occasionally find older Flickas on the used market at half the price of a new one—still

not micro-budget, but more manageable for some of us.

Which Boat for You?

How could I summarize for you all that we've said about these many different kinds of boats? Let's begin by saying that the choice you make will largely be determined by the kind of sailing you plan to do, the number of people you plan to take with you, the waters you plan to sail in, and the distance you will have to travel to get to the water. Let's review the choices from these perspectives.

Boat Type	Kind of Sailing/ Size of Crew	Sailing Conditions	Distance to Travel	Cost
Micro-cruiser	daysails 4 cruises 2 voyages 1	Lakes, bays, rivers most common; fair to moderate winds; a few are capable of ocean sailing	The best choice if you must haul over long distances	Least expensive
Compact cruiser	daysails 4 cruises 2 to 4 voyages 1 to 2	Lakes, bays, rivers most common; fair to moderate winds; a few are capable of ocean sailing	Still light enough to haul and launch fairly easily	More expensive
Open cruiser	daysails up to 6 cruises 2 to 4 extended cruises 1 to 2	Most are designed for inland and coastal sailing in fair to moderate winds	Still light enough to haul and launch easily	More expensive
Family weekender	daysails up to 6 cruises 4 extended cruises 2	Most are designed for comfortable inland and coastal sailing in fair to moderate winds	Portable, but more demanding to trailer and launch	Most expensive
Cruising multihull	daysails 4 to 6 cruises 1 to 2 extended cruises 1 to 2	Mostly designed for high-speed inland and coastal sailing in fair to moderate winds	Portable, but more demanding to trailer and launch	Most expensive
Maxi-trailerable	daysails 4 to 6 cruises 2 to 4 extended cruises 2	Comfortable coastal and inland cruising	Portable, but more demanding to trailer and launch	Most expensive

If I were to identify a single most endearing characteristic of each type, I'll like the micro-cruiser for its wonderful ease of transportation and operation. Everything is so easy.

The compact cruiser is my favorite all-around compromise choice. You can squeeze in a family of four, you can haul it around fairly easily, and the price is still within the reach of most families.

The open cruiser is the most comfortable daysailer of the group because of its open spaciousness. Many are still easily covered over at night. Also, I like the wide choice in designs available.

Family weekenders and maxi-trailerables are wonderful if you can afford them and don't mind the extra work hauling and launching. I've even seen some I could imagine living on for a stretch of time.

The cruising multihull's greatest appeal is its speed. Comfort overnight and portability are only moderately good; it's the sailing that would turn the multihull enthusiast on more than anything else.

One last thing. Some boats just appeal to you because . . . well, they just do. For some reason, they conform to your idea of what a small boat should look like. Personally, I'm attracted by the convertible charms of open cruising boats yet, maybe irrationally, I like a cabin with grabrails on the roof. A cabin means security to me. This is wholly irrational, but there it is. I owned a family weekender once, but got tired of hauling it around and, under sail, found it too big. Nice boat, though . . . lots of room. Evidently, my concept of an ideal boat involves something quite little. Your ideals will be different, of course—wholly unique to you. So browse around a lot; look at lots of pictures; go to as many boat shows as you can; and listen to your irrational heart. Despite all the practical considerations, the boat you see when you close your eyes is the one you really want.

Conclusion

It's a snowy Sunday afternoon. Bored with football, I turn off the set and wander to the window. The storm continues unabated; snow sifts through the trees, rumbles from the roofs, blankets the ground.

Bundled in my coat and boots, I clomp through the kitchen on my way outdoors. A pot steams; my wife looks up. "Going to visit the boat?" I'm continually stunned by how well she knows me.

Outdoors I don't notice the cold so much as the silence. I plow twin furrows to the garage and feel the satisfying crunch under my feet. I pound back a wedge of snow with the garage door and slip inside. All around the edges of the open door, snowflakes flutter and catch the silver light. Inside the garage, sound is muffled. There is *Fearless*, blocked up on the earth floor. Her white decks are dusty and pigeons have spattered her here and there. I slide a gloved hand along her bow. Oddly, when I try to remember summertime voyages, no images come. I peer into the smoked plastic windows but see nothing. A gust of wind buffets the building; snow swirls in through the shaft of light. I let myself out. It's bright. I fasten the latch and tramp, squinting, back to the kitchen door.

"How was it?" my wife asks. My boots are already making puddles on the floor. I step in one, feel the wet cold soaking through my sock and pull my foot back in annoyance. My glasses fog up. "It's OK." Without knowing why, I'm confused. Not knowing why I went out, it's hard to say how it was. Why exactly *did* I go out?

I guess I really wanted to "visit" with my boat, as my wife put it. When we trust our lives to a product of our own hands, maybe we still have that ancient need to believe that the thing has a soul—so we can trust it, talk to it when we get scared, thank it for safe passages. In the age of fiberglass, maybe we need that old superstition more than ever.

It's getting dark now. The streetlight illuminates a cone of falling snow. I lie down to take a nap. As I close my eyes, I imagine it's summer and I'm aboard. In my mind's eye I visualize the cabin. I know where everything is. I know exactly where I can reach out and touch Bettina's shoulder. If I slide open the hatch, I'll have a patch of stars that swing in lazy arcs in and out of view until I'm tranced into sleep. What more could anyone want?

Appendix 1

Trailering Safety Checklist

Whenever you stop for gas, food, or a rest, walk around the car and trailer and check the following:

- Trailer-to-car connection
- Safety chains both hooked on
- Lights connected and working
- Boat tie-down straps secure
- Boat winched up tight onto trailer, handle tied down
- Lug nuts on wheels all tight
- Trailer hitch bolted tightly to car
- Good air pressure in tires

Vibration on the road is a continual source of mischief. Your little trailer wheels spin much faster than your automobile tires.

Things can come loose with amazing speed. To travel safely, you should have the following supplies in your car:

- A lug wrench that fits your trailer's wheels
- A crescent wrench
- Vice-Grip pliers
- A tire pressure gauge
- A spare trailer wheel and tire, inflated for use

Now you can go anywhere. Frequent checking is the key. Whenever you're in doubt about anything, pull over and check. You wouldn't want to lose your boat. Consider the carnage if your trailer disconnected and swerved into oncoming traffic.

Appendix 2

Your Boat's Tool Kit

These are best kept in a small plastic tool or tackle box to prevent rust. We carry the following:

- A hand-powered drill and set of bits
- Needle-nose pliers/wire cutters
- Vice-Grip pliers
- A wrench set
- A small assortment of nuts, bolts, washers, and wood screws

- Phillips-head and slot-head screwdrivers
- A roll of strong wire
- Needle and thread for sail repair
- A plug wrench for the outboard motor
- A spare spark plug

In a separate bag, we carry an assortment of lines tied in neat bundles, plus a bunch of short sections for use as "stops" or tie-downs.

Appendix 3

A Small First-Aid Kit

Many prepackaged first-aid kits are available. We prefer to assemble our own, containing the following items:

- A box of Band-Aids
- Several larger bandages
- Adhesive tape
- An Ace bandage with clips
- A bottle of pain reliever

- Antihistamines
- Antiseptic and lotion for cuts, scrapes, and sunburn
- Cotton swabs
- Scissors
- Insect repellent
- Bug-bite lotion
- Sunscreen lotion for your body and 100-percent sunblock for nose, lips, etc.

Appendix 4

For Safety

- A Coast Guard–approved life jacket for each person on your boat.
- Tie whistles to each life jacket with a short cord.
- For night sailing, clip a small waterproof light to each life jacket.
- At least one throwable life cushion or ring.
- An air horn for signaling.
- Coast Guard–approved running lights for use at night.
- A waterproof flashlight.
- Solid grabrails on the cabin roof and wher ever else handholds are needed. (Remember that a child's reach is not as long as yours.)
- A loop around one of the rudder gudgeons. Better yet, a permanently mounted boarding ladder provides a way to get back on board—especially for someone too young or too old to get back on board by brute force alone.
- A solid point of attachment for a lifeline or a safety harness in foul weather or at night.
- A fire extinguisher.
- Coast Guard–approved rescue flares.
- Keep an adequate anchor ready with at least 150 feet of strong line. Will your cleat or bow eye hold? Reinforce if needed.
- Pumps with hoses long enough to reach into the cabin and to clear it of water.
- Always have a compass. Even a Boy Scout compass is better than nothing.
- Charts for your planned sailing waters.
- Leave a trip itinerary with a friend with instructions to call the Coast Guard if you don't phone in after a reasonable time.
- Check weather reports before setting out.
- Always have first-aid supplies aboard.

Appendix 5

Some Good Reading

Boating Magazines

Sailboat & Equipment Directory, 275 Washington St., Newton, MA 02158-1630

An annual listing with photographs and specs.

Sailboat Buyers Guide, Alan Chappell, Seashore Publications, Long Beach, MS 39560

Photos, line drawings, and information on more than 1,000 sailboats.

Cruising World, 5 John Clarke Road, Newport, RI 02840

The wonderful stuff of which sailing fantasies are made.

SAIL, 275 Washington St., Newton, MA 02158-1630

More racing oriented. Good how-to information, too. A solid general interest publication.

WoodenBoat, P.O. Box 78, Brooklin, ME 04616

Classic taste, beautiful photography. Good information for do-it-yourself builders.

Lakeland Boating, 106 Perry St., Port Clinton, OH 43452

Specializes in freshwater sailing. Useful information for inland cruise planning.

Boatbuilder, P.O. Box 1109, West Palm Beach, FL 33402

Devoted to the interests and needs of kit and scratch boat builders.

Sailing, Port Publications, Inc., 125 E. Main St., P.O. Box 249, Port Washington, WI 53074

A good magazine with a nice design section and an eclectic mix of articles.

General Interest Reading

Some of these book are out of print, but you might be able to find them at the library.

Sea Sense, Third Edition, by Richard Henderson, International Marine, Camden, ME
  If I could own only one book on seamanship, this would be it.

The Elements of Seamanship, by Roger C. Taylor, International Marine, Camden, ME
  A patient and humorous introduction to the basics of sailing.

Trailerable Sailboats, by Chris Caswell, W. W. Norton & Co., Inc., New York, NY
  Deals with boats 20 feet and up. A useful primer. Good photos, too.

Boat Trailers and Tow Vehicles: A User's Guide, by Steve Henkel, International Marine, Camden, ME
  A how-to-do-it manual for worry-free trailering.

Handbook of Sailing, by Bob Bond, Alfred A. Knopf, Inc., New York, NY
  Lucid explanations, diagrams, and photos on how to sail.

Heavy Weather Sailing, Fourth Edition, by K. Adlard Coles, International Marine, Camden, ME
  A thorough treatment of bad-weather tactics and concerns.

Sea Quest, by Charles A. Borden, Ballantine Books, Inc., New York, NY

A dated but marvelous chronicle of various small-boat cruising exploits. Salty and informative.

The Thousand Dollar Yacht, by Anthony Bailey, International Marine, Camden, ME
  A charming, gently humorous account of building a cruising dory.

Handbook of Trailer Sailing, Second Edition, by Robert Burgess, International Marine, Camden, ME
  A useful collection of ideas and how-to tips from an experienced Com-Pac 16 and 19 sailor.

Sailing America, by Larry Brown, International Marine, Camden, ME
  Picks up where the book you're reading leaves off: how to effectively take your small boat on trailer-sailing expeditions, planning, cooking, sleeping, travel tips, safety, good boats, etc. Part 2 inventories North America's sailing regions—what's there, things to know, where to get more information.

Small-Boat Cruising Epics

Sailing Alone Around the World, by Joshua Slocum, Sheridan House, Inc., Dobbs Ferry, NY
  An engaging account of the classic small-boat cruise of all time.

Tinkerbelle, by Robert Manry, Harper & Rowe Publishers, Inc., New York, NY
  About Manry's voyage alone across the Atlantic in his 13-foot boat. Good reading.

Alone Against the Atlantic, by Gary Spiess, Berkely Publishing Group, New York, NY

Excellent narrative with useful details documenting a methodical and thoroughly seamanlike approach to small-boat voyaging.

April Fool, by Hugo Vihlen, Follett Publishing Co., Chicago, IL

An airline pilot decides to cross the Atlantic in the smallest boat ever and survives. An enjoyable book about a sailor who God evidently decided to forgive for his inexperience.

Shrimpy, by Shane Acton, Patrick Stevens Ltd., Cambridge, England

Acton sets sail from England to go around the world in an 18-foot boat. In Panama he teams up with a beautiful Swedish lass and off they go. A light-hearted tale of sailing serendipity and a hymn of praise to small-boat sailing. A large-print edition is available in the U.S. through Ulverscroft, Guilford, CT.

The Incredible Voyage, by Tristan Jones, Avon Books, New York, NY

Jones' voyages in an 18-footer from England to Palestine, then to South America to explore Lake Titicaca. Dead Sea, Titicaca; high water, low water. Salty, irreverent, savvy, fascinating.

Northern Seas, Hardy Sailors, by George Whitely, W. W. Norton & Co., Inc., New York, NY

Written by a man who loves the Canadian maritime coast and its people. Stories of the seagoing life, and often of incredible hardship along this coast. Some harrowing tales of shipwreck, too. Good reading...makes you glad you're safe in your armchair.

Open Boat Across the Pacific, by Webb Chiles, W. W. Norton & Co., Inc., New York, NY

One of a series of books about his epic voyage around the world in a 16-foot open boat—a Drascombe Lugger.

Cruising in Seraffyn, by Lin and Larry Pardey, Seven Seas Press, Camden, ME

Any book by these full-time cruisers will be lively and full of useful pointers.

Boat and Sail Design

American Small Sailing Craft, by Howard I. Chapelle, W. W. Norton & Co., Inc., New York, NY

A superb historical text and a classic review of hulls and sailing rigs.

The Dory Book, by John Gardner, International Marine, Camden, ME

A detailed look at various traditional flat-bottomed working boats and rigs.

Thirty Classic Boat Designs: The Best of the Good Boats, by Roger C. Taylor, International Marine, Camden, ME

Takes long and loving looks at an interesting and eclectic bunch of boats. Taylor has impeccable taste.

Small Boats... Different Boats... The Folding Schooner, by Philip C. Bolger, International Marine, Camden, ME

Anything by Bolger is worth reading. He's maybe the most clever and open-minded boat designer in the country.

100 Small Boat Rigs, by Philip C. Bolger, International Marine, Camden, ME

A how-to guide to rigging. Practical and useful.

The Complete Guide to Boat Kits, Ocean Logic Publications, Inc., West Palm Beach, FL

Lists suppliers of boat kits and components.

The Boat Who Wouldn't Float, by Farley Mowat, Bantam Books, Inc., New York, NY

Hilarious account of fixing up and cruising in a derelict schooner.

Nautical History

Traditions and Memories of American Yachting, by William P. Stephens, International Marine, Camden, ME

Vintage drawings and photographs grace this coffee-table volume.

The Ship, by Björn Landstrom, Doubleday & Co., Inc., New York, NY

Complete history of ships. Exquisite artwork. Any book by Landstrom is a treasure.

Living Aboard

The Complete Live-Aboard Book, by Katy Burke, Seven Seas Press, Camden, ME

Realistic and imaginative pointers based on living aboard a 20-foot Flicka.

Gently with the Tides: The Best of Living Aboard, edited by Michael L. Frankel, International Marine, Camden, ME

Eighteen years' worth of articles submitted to *Living Aboard* journal, along with surveys, provide a rich and detailed picture of the liveaboard lifestyle.

Cookbooks

Cooking on the Go, rev. ed., by Janet Groene, Hearst Books/William Morrow & Co., New York, NY

Lots of hints, tricks, techniques.

First Aid

Advanced First Aid Afloat, Third Edition, by Peter F. Eastman, Cornell Maritime Press, Centreville, MD

A comprehensive guide for cruising and racing sailors without immediate access to medical help.

Appendix 6

Manufacturers of Trailerable Cruising Sailboats

Abbott Boats Limited, 1458 London Rd., Sarnia, Ontario, Canada N7S 1P7; (519) 542-2771. *Abbott 22*.

B-Boats, Inc., 8902 Marylee Dr., Garden Grove, CA 92641; (714) 534-3369. *B-25*.

Beneteau U.S.A., Ltd., 8720 Red Oak Blvd., Suite 102, Charlotte, NC 28217; (704) 527-8244. *Beneteau First 235 (23 feet)*.

Bight Services, Inc., Port Annapolis Marina, 7078 Bembe Beach Rd., Suite 115, Annapolis, MD 21403; (301) 268-2414. *Etap 22i, Etap 24*.

Fred P. Bingham, Yacht Design, 55 N. Broad St. #245, San Luis Obispo, CA 93405; (805) 545-9690. *Bingham 22, Bingham 25*.

C&L Boatworks, 884 Dillingham Rd., Pickering, Ontario, Canada L1W 1N8; (416) 839-7991. *Sandpiper 565 (18 feet)*.

Capital Yachts, Inc., 25914 President Ave., Harbor City, CA 90710; (213) 530-1311. *Neptune 16*.

Catalina Yachts, 21200 Victory Blvd., Woodland Hills, CA 91367; (818) 884-7700. *Capri 16, 18, 22; Catalina 22*.

Classic Yacht Builders, 4301 Johnson Dr., P.O. Box 645, Chanute, KS 66720; (316) 431-4331. *Gloucester 19, Gloucester 20, Gloucester 22*.

Corsair Marine, 150 Center St., Chula Vista, CA 92011; (619) 585-3005. *F-27 Trimaran*.

Custom Fiberglass Products of Florida, Inc., 8136 Leo Kidd Ave., Port Richey,

FL 34668; (813) 847-5798. *Antares 17, Sovereign 18, Sovereign 20, Sovereign 24, Express 19 Weekender, Peep Hen 14, Mud Hen 17, Bay Hen 21.*

Devlin Designing Boat Builders, 2424 Gravelly Beach Loop NW, Olympia, WA 98502; (206) 866-0164. *Nancy's China (15 feet), Seagull 19.*

Dockrell Yachts, Ltd., 1839 Route 46, Parsippany, NJ 07054; (201) 334-5100. *Dockrell 22, Dockrell 27.*

Edey & Duff, Ltd., 128 Aucoot Rd., Mattapoisett, MA 02739; (508) 758-2743. *Dovekie (21 feet), Shearwater (28 feet).*

Gordon Douglas Boat Company, Route 4, Box K-9, Cemetery Lane, Deer Park, MD 21550; (301) 334-4848. *Flying Scot (19 feet).*

Halman Manufacturing Company, P.O. Box 659, Durham Rd., Beamsville, Ontario, Canada L0R 1B0; (416) 945-6666. *Henley 20, Halman 21, Shark 24.*

Helton Marine, 1763 Topside Rd., Louisville, TN 37777. *Solo II (17 feet).*

HMS Marine, Inc., 904 West Hyde Park Blvd., Inglewood, CA 90302; (213) 674-4540. *West Wight Potter 15, West Wight Potter 19.*

Hobie Cat, 4925 Oceanside Blvd., Oceanside, CA 92056; 1-800-456-2628. *Sportcruiser (18 feet).*

Hunter Marine Corporation, P.O. Box 1030, Route 441, Alachua, FL 32615; (904) 462-3077. *Hunter 18.5, Hunter 23.*

Hutchins Co., Inc., 1195 Kapp Dr., Clearwater, FL 34625; (813) 443-4408. *Com-Pac 16/2, Com-Pac 19/3, Com-Pac 23/3.*

Impulse Marine, Inc., 10610 Metric Dr. #145, Dallas, TX 75243; (214) 340-3111. *Impulse 21.*

International Yachting Center, U.S. 64 West, P.O. Box 166, Columbia, NC 27925; (919) 796-0435. *Sunbeam 23.*

Jeanneau North America, 32 Place De La Gare, 59000 Lille, France; 011-33-20-06823. *Jeanneau Sun Way 21, Jeanneau Tonic 23.*

Johnson Boat Works, 4495 Lake Ave., White Bear Lake, MN 55110; (612) 429-7221. *Johnson Weekender 18.*

MacGregor Yacht Corporation, 1631 Placentia, Costa Mesa, CA 92627; (714) 642-6830. *MacGregor 19 and 26.*

Marine Concepts, 159 Oakwood St. E, Tarpon Springs, FL 34689; (813) 937-0166. *Sea Pearl 21, Rob Roy 23-S, Sea Pearl 28.*

Marshall Marine, Box P, 266 Shipyard Lane, South Dartmouth, MA 02748; (508) 994-0414. *Marshall 18.*

Menger Boatworks, Inc., 121 Maple Ave., Bayshore, NY 11706; (516) 968-0300. *Menger Cat 15, Menger Cat 19.*

Moore Sailboats, 1650 Commercial Way, Santa Cruz, CA 95065; (408) 476-3839. *Moore 24 SC.*

Newport R&D, Inc., 2 Harborview Dr., Newport, RI 02840; (401) 849-3997. *Caravel 22.*

Nimble Boats, Inc., 6135 142nd Ave. N, Clearwater, FL 34620; (813) 539-6444. *Nimble 20, Nimble 24, Nimble 25, Nimble 25, Arctic 25 (now Kodiak 25).*

Nor'Sea Marine, P.O. Box 14, Dana Point, CA 92629; (714) 855-8344. *Nor'Sea 27.*

Outrigger Boat Company, 2142 North Magnolia, Chicago, IL 60614; (312) 477-7413. *Somersault 26.*

Pacific Seacraft, 1301 E. Orangethorpe, Fullerton, CA 92631; (714) 879-1601. *Flicka 20.*

Pearson Yachts, W. Shore Rd., Portsmouth, RI 02871; (401) 683-0100. *O'Day 240.*

Precision Boat Works, 1511 18th Ave. Dr. E, Palmetto, FL 34221; (813) 722-6601. *Precision 18, Precision 21, Precision 23.*

Quickstep, Inc., 17 Broad Common Rd., Bristol, RI 02809; (401) 254-0400. *Quickstep 19, Quickstep 21, Quickstep 24.*

Sea Wind Catamaran Sales, Inc., P.O. Box 36, Indian Rocks Beach, FL 34635; (813) 573-4477. *Sea Wind 24 Catamaran.*

Starboard Yacht Company, 4550 SE Hampton Ct., Stuart, FL 34997; (407) 286-7170. *Seaward Sea Fox (17 feet), Seaward 23, Seaward 25.*

Stuart Marine, P.O. Box 469, 38 Gordon Dr., Rockport, ME 04841; (207) 594-5515. *Mariner 19.*

Super Ray Sailboats, 1150 19th St. N, St. Petersburg, FL 33713; (813) 822-7663. *SR Max (21 feet).*

Tremolino Boat Company, 411 South Sixth St., Chaska, MN 55318; (612) 448-6855. *Tremolino II Trimaran (22 feet), Tremolino Argonauta Trimaran (25 feet).*

Index

If you enjoyed *Frugal Yachting,* you might be interested in these International Marine books. Prices are subject to change.

Boatowner's Energy Planner: How to Make and Manage Electrical Energy on Board
Kevin and Nan Jeffrey

A detailed exploration of onboard energy systems, including marine alternators, portable generators, solar panels, wind and water generators, battery management, AC shore-power hookups, and system controls and accessories for both DC and AC electrical service, with just enough theory to make all the options crystal clear. "A valuable addition to any boat maintenance library."   —*Offshore*

Paperbound, 288 pages, 77 illustrations, $21.95.
ISBN No. 0-915160-63-3

Spurr's Boatbook: Upgrading the Cruising Sailboat, Second Edition
Dan Spurr

A revised and expanded edition of the best-selling stem-to-stern, project-by-project approach to improving any sailboat for safe and comfortable coastal or offshore cruising. "Its crisp style, clarity of detail and excellent source references should ensure it a place in any nautical library."   —*Sailing*

Paperbound, 352 pages, 422 illustrations, $24.95.
ISBN No. 0-87742-411-X

Boating for Less: How to Save Money When Buying, Owning, and Selling Your Power or Sail Boat, Second Edition
Steve Henkel

An indispensable guide, whether you're a first-time buyer of a small boat or a boatowner trading up to a larger yacht. "There is so much solid information in this book that it's difficult to imagine how anyone who studies it can fail to derive a return many times its modest cost."

—*Sail*

Paperbound, 320 pages, 60 illustrations, $19.95.
ISBN No. 0-87742-315-6

The Complete Canvasworker's Guide: How to Outfit Your Boat with Fabric, Second Edition
Jim Grant

A thorough, step-by-step guide to making all common items of fabric boat gear, including boat covers, bags, sail covers, bosun's chairs, cushions, dodgers, bimini tops, flags, hatch covers, and much more. This new edition is larger by half than the universally praised first edition.

Paperbound, 224 pages, 230 illustrations, $19.95.
ISBN No. 0-87742-335-0

Gently with the Tides: The Best of Living Aboard
Edited by Michael L. Frankel

Fueled by 18 years of letters and articles from *Living Aboard* journal and the results of hundreds of surveys, *Gently with the Tides* is a powerful testimonial to the lure of living aboard. It includes information about why people move aboard—and why some move back ashore, the "perfect" boat, galley and provisioning hints, the law and live-aboard rights, and much more. "A must for anyone seeking insights into the wonderful world of the liveaboard."   —*Heartland Boating*

Paperbound, 240 pages, 22 illustrations, $14.95.
ISBN No. 0-87742-375-X

The Nature of Boats: Insights and Esoterica
for the Nautically Obsessed
Dave Gerr

   The Nature of Boats is the ideal companion for old salts, boatyard crawlers, boatshow oglers, and landlocked dreamers. It's packed with understandable explanations of the difference between initial and reserve stability, of how torque and horsepower work, of traditional boatbuilding materials versus high-tech, of rudder control, of speed powered by sails versus engines, of flotation and trim. Dave Gerr examines sail and power boats from every conceivable angle to create a book that's not only fascinating and fun, but also extremely useful.

"Fascinating potpourri of information about today's boats, modern and traditional; reminiscent of the work of Culler, Lane, Davis, Atkin, and many others of an earlier era."   —*WoodenBoat*

"Gerr understands those of us afflicted with a passion for boats. Furthermore he trades on our insatiable appetites for nautical tidbits. And he does it well. Gerr has a talent for describing complicated concepts in simple terms."   —*SEA*

Hardbound, 432 pages, 253 illustrations, $29.95.
ISBN No. 0-87742-289-3

Boat Trailers and Tow Vehicles: A User's Guide
Steve Henkel

Densely illustrated with Steve Henkel's clear drawings, *Boat Trailers and Tow Vehicles* is packed with information showing adjustment, towing, launching, maintenance, and repair procedures. It describes how to choose the right style and type of trailer for a particular boat and trailering venue; how to choose the best tow vehicle; how to troubleshoot and repair the electrics and wheel bearings; how to correct sway and stability problems while towing; and much more. Detailed appendices include trailer towing regulations by state; trailer towing ratings for cars, vans, and pickups; and a product source list.

"A book like this has been long needed. . . . [It covers] subjects that often take boaters several years to learn. It's a good investment."
—*Trailer Boats*

"The best single source guide I've seen. Commonsense advice, and nicely organized." —*American Sailor*

"A no fluff practical primer that can help the trailer boater steer a safe course along the highways to the high seas." —*Sailing*

Paperbound, 144 pages, 50 illustrations, $14.95.
ISBN No. 0-87742-290-7

**Look for These and Other International Marine Books
at Your Local Bookstore**

To Order, Call Toll Free 1-800-822-8158
or Write to International Marine/TAB Books
A Division of McGraw-Hill, Inc.
Blue Ridge Summit, PA 17294-0840.

- -

Title	Product No.	Quantity Price

Subtotal: $_____

Postage and Handling
($3.00 in U.S., $5.00 outside U.S.): $_____

Add applicable state and local sales tax: $_____

TOTAL: $_____

❑ Check or money order made payable to TAB Books

Charge my ❑ VISA ❑ MasterCard ❑ American Express

Acct. No.: _____ Exp.: _____

Signature: _____

Name: _____

Address: _____

City: _____

State: _____ Zip: _____

Orders outside U.S. must pay with international money order in U.S. dollars.

**If for any reason you are not satisfied with the book(s) you order, simply
return it (them) within 15 days and receive a full refund.**